Delaware & Maryland Beaches

1905-1965

Lee Dixon

Schiffer Publishing Ltd

4880 Lower Valley Road, Atglen, Pennsylvania 19310

Dedication

This book is dedicated to my niece, Dannarae, who has anterograde amnesia, a condition that precludes new memories from being stored in the brain. She's my daily reminder that our ability to recall the happy moments of our lives is a gift from God that we all too often take for granted.

Published by Schiffer Publishing Ltd.
4880 Lower Valley Road
Atglen, PA 19310
Phone: (610) 593-1777; Fax: (610) 593-2002
E-mail: Info@schifferbooks.com

Designed by Mark David Bowyer
Type set in Schneidler Blk BT / Souvenir Lt BT
ISBN: 978-0-7643-2753-7

Printed in China

For the largest selection of fine reference books on this and related subjects, please visit our web site at *www.schifferbooks.com*
We are always looking for people to write books on new and related subjects. If you have an idea for a book please contact us at the above address.

This book may be purchased from the publisher.
Include $3.95 for shipping.
Please try your bookstore first.
You may write for a free catalog.

In Europe, Schiffer books are distributed by
Bushwood Books
6 Marksbury Ave.
Kew Gardens
Surrey TW9 4JF England
Phone: 44 (0) 20 8392-8585; Fax: 44 (0) 20 8392-9876
E-mail: info@bushwoodbooks.co.uk
Website: www.bushwoodbooks.co.uk
Free postage in the U.K., Europe; air mail at cost.

Acknowledgments

Thanks to Dinah Roseberry and Tina Skinner at Schiffer Publishing for their enthusiasm for this project. It was their suggestion that I assemble and publish my collection which ultimately led to the creation of this book. Dinah, as editor, then went on to coax me through numerous revisions. Her signature joviality made the task much less tedious. Additionally, thank you to Sue in Schiffer's design department. The problem of what to put in was quickly overwhelmed by the bigger problem of what to leave out. Thanks, too, to Lollie, my gracious wife of 28 years, sorted, separated, and critiqued postcards with me until we had them winnowed down to "only" 460 or 470 different cards. Thanks, too, for her tireless reading of messages on the backs as we sought out the most interesting of those among thousands. Mary, Joey, Donna, and "Mr. Bill" at Mary Martin, LTD. Postcards in Perryville, MD were generous hosts for a long afternoon of reading the backs of boxes full of postcards. Those folks are a class act.

Special thanks to Bob Fisher of Snow Hill, a dealer in postcards and a good friend. His Ocean City collection is quite extensive. On one visit he appointed himself stenographer so I could focus completely on reading the backs of postcards. The name Fisher in Ocean City is synonymous with the very best caramel popcorn on the boardwalk. You guessed it, same family. To pro photographer Nick Varrato for use of his classic Nomad Village view, thanks. Nick is an avid postcard collector, a nice guy, and I'm pleased to call him friend.

Lastly, to the Moms, Grandpas, Aunts, friends, co-workers, and happy recipients of all the postcards since that first one left the coastal beach resorts of Delaware and Maryland so long ago—we tip our hat. You inspired someone to share their experience on the back of a postcard. Today, in the twenty-first century, we get to re-live those moments.

Contents

How To Use This Book

If "a picture is worth a thousand words," then without them, this book would need to be about 900 pages. Already, you have a better appreciation for good illustrations, right?

Text has been sparingly added to this postcard "scrapbook" for three purposes.

1. On old labels, to convey some card titles, to offer additional information that was printed on the reverse, or to highlight a bit of light historical info.

2. On the small caption lines along the top or bottom edge of each card to offer important information. These lines contain:

A. Reference number — assigned for future reference to the cards in this book.

B. Date — estimation of the era in which a card was printed which may include:

a) The postmark, if it has one with a legible date.

b) CT production code date. (CT is short for Curt Teich of Chicago, a large producer of postcards for more than 50 years, often for other publishers.)

c) Circa date e. g. "c.1910" meaning around this time period.

C. Publisher — if known.

D. Price range; what you might expect to pay a knowledgeable dealer for a similar card in really good condition. Heavy creases, excessive corner or edge wear, and small tears can detract considerably from this value depending on the rarity of the card.

3. On tan colored notes pasted here and there with messages from senders to show the real life "Echoes from the Shore."

If the pictures are the heart of this book, the messages are its soul.

Some are placed in relation to their content. Most are pretty much timeless in their appeal. Along with the images they've been chosen to accent, they reach out to connect us with the light hearted fun times that beach lovers know so well. Enjoy!

THE OCEAN AND ME

36346

Greetings from Ocean City, Md.

Introduction

You love the beach. You always have. You share that with millions who went before you. You'll pass it on to those that come after.

Those who came before you first sought recreation and respite on the coastal waters of Delaware and Maryland in the late 1800s. They fell in love and made their way back again and again. They came by horse and buggy. They came on steamships and trains and planes. They came in motorcars that started by hand crank.

They had too much fun to keep it a secret, so they sent postcards ... by the millions. "Having a great time, wish you were here" became the mantra of generation after generation of happy beachgoers.

Through World Wars and depression, from the industrial revolution to the space age, in good times and in bad, postcards from the beach form a whimsical narrative of magical times enjoyed.

The book in your hands is not a history book, though it is filled with historical images. It's not a graphical arts book, yet the artistic medium of the postcard, whether by camera or brush, can't be denied. It's not just a collector book, though it should become a valuable resource for local postcard enthusiasts.

What you hold is an image scrapbook of life in a simpler time ...a silent appeal from beach lovers over the years to preserve the memory of what they held so dear.

Dropped here and there like random seashells in the sand you'll find their words to family and friends, authentic, both in context and feeling.

Listen as you look and you'll hear their thoughts.

"We worked and played here. We laughed and cried. We ate and drank ... danced and sang. We built sand castles too."

"Though time and change separate us, our memories live on in the hearts and minds of all who embrace the romance of the seashore."

Be it the sun caressing the horizon at daybreak, going barefoot in the sand at noon, or strolling the night away on a moonlit beach to the rhythmic sound of the surf, the mystical allure of the coast outlives us all.

Augustine Beach

Augustine Beach, located on the Delaware River just south of Port Penn, was once described as "The Coney Island of Delaware. Famous for Bathing, Fishing, Boating and Picnic Grove."

DANCING PAVILLION AUGUSTINE BEACH, DEL.

#1001—c. 1910, publisher unknown, $15-20

#1002—postmarked 1910, publisher unknown, $20-25

#1003—postmarked 1909, Ed Herbener "Best" series, $10-15

BATHING SCENE, AUGUSTINE BEACH, DEL.

Bathing Scene with side-wheel steamer Thomas Clyde at the pier.

The Delaware River Steamer Thomas Clyde brought excursionists to Augustine Beach from Philadelphia.

A 1,765 ft. Artesian Well.

HOTEL, AUGUSTINE BEACH, DEL.

#1005-postmarked 1915, publisher unknown, $15-20

176\5 FT. ARTESIAN WELL, AUGUSTINE BEACH, DEL.

#1004 - postmarked 1910 publisher unknown, $15-20

Beach Pavilion.

#1006-postmarked 1911, publisher unknown, $15-20

PAVILION. AUGUSTINE BEACH, DEL.

"The House of Famous Bands at Augustine Beach."

GLOBE BALLROOM - AUGUSTINE BEACH, DELAWARE

#1007- c. 1910, National Press, Chicago, $25-30

#1008-postmarked 1911, publisher unknown. $25-30

MERRY GO-ROUND, AUGUSTINE BEACH, DEL.

#1009—c. 1910, publisher unknown, $30-35

MINIATURE R. R., AUGUSTINE BEACH, DEL.

Smaller Delaware Beaches
Deemer Beach – near New Castle, Delaware

DEEMER BEACH BATH HOUSE, DEEMER BEACH PARK, NEW CASTLE COUNTY, DELAWARE

#2002—c. 1910, Deemer Beach Corp., New Castle, Del., $35-50

#2003—c. 1910, Deemer Beach Corp., New Castle, Del., $35-50

#2004—c.1910, Deemer Beach Corp., New Castle, Del., $35-50

DEEMER BEACH PARK, NEW CASTLE COUNTY, DELAWARE

PICNIC WOODS, DEEMER BEACH PARK, NEW CASTLE COUNTY, DELAWARE

Woodland Beach

WOODLAND BEACH, DEL.

#2005—postmarked 1906, publisher unknown, $15-20

#2006—c.1906, publisher unknown, $10-15

HOTEL AT WOODLAND BEACH DEL.

#2007—c.1906, publisher unknown, $15-20

From a postcard postmarked 1927:

"Woodland Beach has been a most popular summer resort for more than fifty years due to its fine Bathing, Fishing, Hotel, and Shaded Picnic Grounds. The Beach is located six miles from Symrna, Delaware, which is on the DuPont-Delmarva trail, from New York to Miami, Florida."

1937 message to Mrs. Hawkins,

"am down here having a good time Crabbing and Fishing. This place is about 80 miles south of Phila. Have been feeling fine and hope you are the same. Love, Leon and Olive"

Woodland Beach Park—Beach Motel—Cabins and Cottages—near the boardwalk and shaded grove—free parking—Sportsman's vacation wonder land—Bathing—Boating—Crabbing and Fishing—Complete restaurant service—Sea food a specialty—Nite Club.

BATHING IN DELAWARE BAY, WOODLAND BEACH, DEL.

Kitts Hummock

1912 message to Minnie,

"Hello! We're at Kitts Hummock and having the grandest time possible. You should just hear the trash that grandpa is telling me today. Love, Eloise Peach"

#2011—postmarked 1912, publisher unknown, $75+

#2012—photograph, dated 1940, $15-20

Slaughter Beach

Slaughter Beach—Mispillion River Lighthouse, built 1873, replaced with steel tower 1929, damaged by fire in 2002 and later removed.

Broadkiln Beach

Oliver C. Beideman and Son

GOOD BATHING
GOOD FISHING
BOATS FOR RENT

B A I T
SQUID
CLAMS
MUSSELS
ETC.

· · · ·

GROCERIES
SOFT DRINKS
CANDY
ICE CREAM
CIGARETTES
TOBACCO
LITE LUNCH

Broadkiln Beach · Milton, Delaware

#2013—c. 1920, publisher unknown, $25-35

Bowers Beach

Kent Cottage.—Bowers Beach, Del.

#3003—postmarked 1908, publisher unknown, $30-40

Main Street and Hubbard Avenue.—Bowers Beach, Del.

#3001—postmarked 1908, publisher unknown, $30-40

#3002—postmarked 1909, Phila. Post Card Co. for Williams & Co., $25-35

1908 message to George,

"pretty decent place and fine people"

3576   Street View, Bowers Beach, Del.

No. 3560   Hubbert Ave., Bowers, Del.

#3004—postmarked 1908, Phila. Post Card Co. for Clara J. Candler, $20-25

No. 3550   Frederica Boat Landing, Bowers, Del.

#3005—postmarked 1908, Phila. Post Card Co. for Clara J. Candler, $20-25

1909 message to Charles,

"Last night I went to a moving picture show with a crowd of eight. They even have a pool room here so Bowers isn't so slow after all. All kinds of amusements here. The bay was awfully rough last night. Laura"

Victorian Women at Boardwalk.

#3007—postmarked 1906, Phila. Post Card Co., $25-35

Bowers Beach—Bowers, Del.

No. 1015.

#3006—postmarked 1907, Phila. Post Card Co. $15-20

River Front—Bowers, Del.

No. 1014.

Post Office, Bowers Beach, Delaware.

#3008—c. 1910, Eureka Post Card Co., Wilmington, Del., $30-40

1912 message to Mrs. Bentz,

"Enjoying everything immensely. This is the nicest little Beach. Had a lovely trip down on the boat."

1910 message to Ella,

"am having the best time of my life here … came to use the salt air as a tonic. Elizabeth"

#3010—postmarked 1921, Auburn Post Card Mfg. Co., Auburn, Ind., $25-35

Landing of the Str. Fredericka, Bowers Beach, Del.

#3009—postmarked 1922, Auburn Post Card Mfg. Co., Auburn, Ind., $10-15

Big Thursday at Bowers Beach

#3012—postmarked 1920, Auburn Post Card Mfg. Co., Auburn, Ind., $10-15

#3013—postmarked 1912, publisher unknown, $25-35

Main Street showing delivery wagon on left for "Royal Quality Bread."

Bay view showing Merry-Go-Round.

#3011 - c. 1920, Auburn Post Card Mfg. Co., Auburn, Ind., $30-40

1915 message,

"Dear Ma, We went up the week—fishing today—caught 4 eels. Jean broke her specks fighting skeeters. It rained hard this morning. Very cold, wind blowing a gale. I am well. Feel Fine. Charles"

Steamer "Frederica" of Frederica, Bower's Beach, Del.

#3015—c. 1910, World Post Card Co., Philadelphia, Pa., $25-35

1912 message to Roy,

"Be home Wednesday as far as I know now. I suppose you'll meet me at the boat. I think it will be there around 7 or 7:30. Mary"

Steamer Frederica.

#3014—postmarked 1909, Williams & Co., $20-25

#3016—c. 1910, processor unknown., $25-35

THE JOHNSON HOTEL, BOWERS BEACH, DEL.   Pub. by Williams & Co.

#3017—postmarked 1919, Clara J. C. Coles, Bowers, Delaware, $20-25

1909 message to Mrs. Taylor,

"Just returned from a launch trip about 25 miles in the bay. Oh! My! But it was rough, but grand. Helen"

Murderkill Ave., Bowers, Delaware, before it was destroyed by fire, December 5, 1913.

Sailing on the Murderkill River.

#3018—c. 1910, for C. J. Candler by Rosin & Co., Phila. & New York, Made in Germany, $15-20

1909 message to Mrs. Palmer,

"Tell pop I have some shark bones for him."

Bowers Bathing Beauties from the Flapper Era.

Greetings from BOWERS, DEL.

#3019—postmarked 1928, Made in U.S.A., publisher unknown, $10-12

1919 message to Edward,

"Spend the days fishing and crabbing in the Delaware Bay. It sure is great fun. Caught a big trout. The mosquitoes, too, are plentiful and bite better than the fish. Best Wishes, Bunnie"

1925 message to Miss Marjorie,

"This is a picture of the kind of fish that 'I intend' to catch tomorrow. Clare"

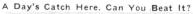

Greetings from BOWERS BEACH, DEL.

#3020—postmarked 1930, Made in USA, publisher unknown, $10-15

#3021—postmarked 1925, Made in USA, publisher unknown, $15-20

#3022—postmarked 1921, Auburn Post Card Mfg. Co., Auburn, Ind., $10-15

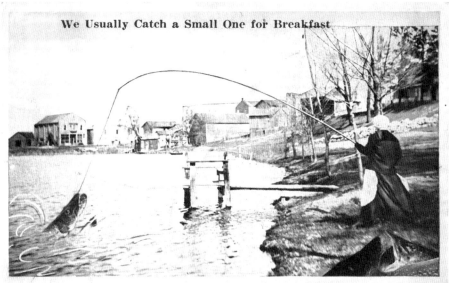

Greetings from BOWERS, DEL.

Greetings from BOWERS, DEL.

Lighthouses of Delaware and Delaware Bay

LEDGE LIGHTHOUSE,
DELAWARE BAY

Mahon River Lighthouse, Port Mahon, Delaware, east of Dover. Long abandoned by the Coast Guard, the Light at Port Mahon was lost to fire in 1984.

SHIP JOHN LIGHT, Delaware Bay.   Hand Colored

Ship John Shoal Light, built 1874, still in active use.

Cross Ledge Lighthouse, Delaware Bay, out of service in 1910, demolished 1962.

Liston Range Rear Light Station, built in 1877, still in active use.

#4004—postmarked 1909, real photo by W. Monro, Middletown, Del., $100+

#4005—c. 1910, Hugh C. Leighton, Portland, Me., Made in Germany, $50+

Fourteen Foot Bank Light, Delaware Bay, built 1888, still in active use.

New Light Station, Harbor of Refuge.

#4006—postmarked 1909, A. Gutowitz, Lewes, Del., $60+

Harbor of Refuge Lighthouse, built in 1908, later storm damaged, demolished in 1925, replaced in 1926 with existing Harbor of Refuge Light.

#4007—c. 1906, O. S. Bunnell, Philadelphia, Pa., $30-40

#4008—c. 1910, Nomis Mfg. Co., N.Y.C., $30-40

Delaware Breakwater, East End Light, showing man on platform.

Delaware Breakwater Light, East End, Delaware Bay.

#4009—c. 1910, Hugh C. Leighton, Portland, Me. Made in Germany, $50+

LIGHT HOUSE ON EAST END OF BREAKWATER,
Lewes, Del.

23

Cape Henlopen Light House.

7 V to M V Rehoboth
Sept 28 - 1908

#4011-postmarked 1908, Murray & Martin, (Germany), $50+

Maritime Exchange at Delaware Breakwater, located on west end of Delaware Breakwater, used as a lighthouse until 1901, became a reporting and signal station for the Philadelphia Maritime Exchange, later used by the Coast Guard, torn down in 1960.

Cape Henlopen Light House, built in 1767, shifting sands around the foundation made it unsafe, abandoned 1924, fell into the sea April 13, 1926.

#4012—c. 1910, Ess an Ess Photo Co., New York, N. Y., $20-25

#4010—postmarked 1907, Murray & Martin, Hand Colored, $60+

1909 message from Lewes to Connecticut on back of early Henlopen Light postcard (sent by a sailor?),

"Hello! the reverse side shows first point of land we saw for three days, letter to follow, Alfonso"

HAND-COLORED

CAPE HENLOPEN LIGHT, Lewes, Del.

#4014—postmarked 1906, photo processor unknown, $100+

Cape Henlopen Lighthouse,
Real Photo showing light
keeper.

FENWICK ISLAND LIGHT HOUSE AND KEEPERS HOMES.

#4015—postmarked 1915, publisher unknown, $50+

Fenwick Island Light House and
Keeper House, built in 1858,
still in active use.

#4013—postmarked 1907, J. M. Vessels, Lewes, Del., $60+

FENWICK ISLAND LIGHTHOUSE, FENWICK ISLAND, MD.

#4016—postmarked 1948, The Collotype Co., Elizabeth, N.J. and N.Y., $15-20

Cape Henlopen Lighthouse, Lewes, Del.

Lewes

A beautifully done hand colored version of the Second Street real photo shown below.

#5001—postmarked 1908, Murray & Martin, Hand Colored, $25-30

Second Street Real Photo showing D. H. Parks Ice Cream & Confectionery.

A 1908 view of Second Street showing both the hand-colored version and the real photo from which it was made.

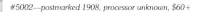

#5002—postmarked 1908, processor unknown, $60+

King Street, Lewes, Del.

#5003—postmarked 1912, Louis Kaufman & Sons, Baltimore, Md., $10-15

Hotel Rodney, Lewes, Del.

#5004—postmarked 1910, A. Gutowitz, Lewes, Del., $20-25

1912 message to Mrs. Smith,

"I am down to the beach. I think the others have all gone to bed but Aunt Mag and she is working in the kitchen. Hope you are well. How is my garden? Lovingly, Mama"

#5005—postmarked 1928, Louis Kaufman & Sons, Baltimore, Md., $30-40

U. S. Life Saving Station, Lewes, Del.

U. S. LIFE SAVING STATION

27

1911 message to Carl,

"Dear Brother   I have been very busy. I left the hotel in July. Am getting all the work I can do. Hope you are well. From Will"

A very fine example of an early "men at work" real photo.

January 1910 message to Lettie,

"Well have you overed the snow storm yet? We are pretty well snowed under down here. Our Xmas entertainment will be held tomorrow night if nothing prevents. Love to little Sara"

PHOTO BY MAX H. KIRSCHT.
PHOTOGRAPHER
PLEASANTVILLE, N. J.

Engine Used to Carry Fish to Boilers - New Lewes Fisheries Co
LEWES, DELAWARE.

#5006—postmarked 1911, Photo by Max H. Kirscht, Photographer, Pleasantville, N. J., $250+

Ocean House.

#5008—postmarked 1931, Kaufman & Sons, Baltimore, Md., $20-25

SOUTH ST., LEWES BEACH.

#5007—c. 1910, for A. Gutowitz by Louis Kaufman & Sons, Baltimore, Md., $30-40

2ND STREET LEWES DEL

1931

Fishing on the Stone Pile, Lewes, Del.

#5009—postmarked 1910, Horn's, Rehoboth, Del., Made in Germany, $10-15

#5011—postmarked 1909, A. Gutowitz, Lewes, Del., Printed in Germany, $10-15

Fort of 1812, Lewes, Del.

#5010—c. 1910, Louis Kaufman & Sons, Baltimore, Md., $15-20

"The Old Fort," Lewes, Del.

Fishing on the Stone Pile, Lewes, Del.

The Breakwater, Lewes, Del.

1910 message to Sarah,

"My Dear Girl, We left Georgetown yesterday for Lewes. We are having a nice time. Gove and his brother have gone out driving this morning. I wish you could be here. The country is so beautiful. Love to all, Maggie"

Fish Boats, Delaware Breakwater, Lewes, Del.

#5012—c. 1910, Louis Kaufman & Sons, Baltimore, Md., $10-15

A WRECK, LEWES BEACH.

#5015—postmarked 1912, for A. Gutowitz by Louis Kaufman & Sons, Baltimore, Md., $25-30

#5014—c. 1910, for A. Gutowitz by Louis Kaufman & Sons, Baltimore, Md., $15-20

#5013—c. 1906, publisher unknown, $15-20

Pilot Boat, Lewes, Del.

TRANSPORTATION PIER, LEWES, DEL.

Where we Bathe, Lewes, Del.

#5017—c. 1910, A. Gutowitz, Jeweler & Optician, Lewes, Del., Printed in Germany, $15-20

Transportation Pier with Steamer.

#5016—postmarked 1915, Louis Kaufman & Sons, Baltimore, Md., $20-25

Transportation Pier, Lewes Beach, Del.

Lewes Canal, Lewes Anglers Association Club House and Boats in background   Lewes, Delaware

#5018—c. 1940, for Arthur H. Morris, Pharmacist, Lewes, Delaware by The Albertype Co., Brooklyn, N.Y., $10-12

Lewes Anglers Club.

1958 message to Eva,

"Daddy just rescued a tremendous 2 lb. turtle crossing the street. He had yellow and orange stripes and red eyes and a green shell. We put him in the Henlopen River. Love Mom"

1952 message to Mr. & Mrs. Ballard,

"Have had quite a bit of fresh fish right out of the sea. Bought it from the men as they pull the boats in. They taste so good. We came for a few days, but this is our second week. Best wishes, Mary, Femmie, and Kitts"

#5022—c. 1960, Rogers Record and Photo Shop, Rehoboth Beach, Del., $8-10

Derrickson's Soda Fountain.

1964 message to Mrs. Nutting,

"Gorgeous weather now. Had to come home 2 nites because of impending hurricane. Love, Jan & Lon"

1950 message to Jean,

"Dear Jean, I am having a very nice time. We have been invited to a hot dog roast tonight by the people next door & the girl asked me to go swimming with she & her friends this afternoon. We have been going to Rehoboth evenings. Love, Joan"

Lewes, Del. — Cape May, N. J. Ferry Service

#5023—c. 1964, Color by J. Paul Rodgers, Dexter Press, West Nyack, N. Y., $8-10

The Cape Henlopen holds 1,200 passengers and 80 cars. The 16-mile trip across the Delaware Bay takes seventy minutes.

#5024—c. 1966, E. Farthing, Rehoboth Beach, Del., $3-5

33

Rehoboth

Rehoboth Rapid Transit Real Photo—taken in front of Horn's Pavilion—1905.

#6002—postmarked 1905, processor unknown, $200+

#6001-c. 1910, processed AZO, $30-40

Cute as a Button Baby and Wicker Cart Real Photo by Pavilion Studio, Voelker & Curran, Prop'rs.

Beach Scene Real Photo.

#6003—postmarked 1905, processor unknown, $75+

#6004—postmarked 1928, processor unknown, $60+

#6006-postmarked 1906, publisher unknown, $20-25

Horn's Pavilion Pier Real Photo showing sign for Horn's Ice Cream on pier.

1906 message to Miss Mary Taylor,

"Hello! Kid. Am having a great time. Certainly wish you were here. Dave"

Horn's Pavilion Backs

Henlopen Light House—Form 1. (bottom left)
The Beach by Night & Day—Form 2. (bottom middle)
A Summer Girl Graphic—Form 3. (top right)
Henlopen Light House—green tint. (bottom right)

#6009—postmarked 1906, Horn's Pavilion, Rehoboth, Delaware

A SUMMER GIRL, REHOBOTH, DEL.

#6007—postmarked 1906, Horn's Pavilion, Rehoboth, Delaware

Collectors Note:

Among the early postcards from Horn's Pavilion, the Night and Day printed backs are the most frequently seen. Lighthouse backs are more scarce and cards showing the Summer Girl are difficult to find.

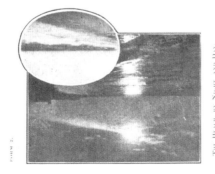

#6008—hand dated 1906, Horn's Pavilion, Rehoboth, Delaware

#6010—postmarked 1912, Horn's Pavilion—green tint, $75+

THE BREAKWATER
REHOBOTH, DEL.
2 MILES LONG, COST $10,000,000. BEHIND WHOSE MASSIVE STONE WALLS THOUS-
ANDS OF SHIPS FIND A SAFE HARBOR.

#6012—c. 1906, Horn's Pavilion,
Rehoboth, Delaware, $30-40

Collector's Note:

Horn's Pavilion was the dominating force in early Rehoboth postcards. Illustrated are three different graphical backs known to be in use as of 1906. Also shown are two alternate ink colors and the Cape Hemlopen Lighthouse in two variations; with and without light keepers present.

As they become increasingly difficult to find, the interesting back styles, alternate ink colors, and subtle scene variations found in these early Horn's Pavilion cards have earned them a special niche with Delaware Postcard collectors.

Lonesome—Horn's Pavilion—Pink Tint (bottom right)
The Breakwater—Horn's Pavilion—vertical title (top left)
Cape Henlopen Light House--Horn's Pavilion--no light keeper (bottom left)

6011—c. 1906, Horn's Pavilion, Rehoboth, Delaware, $30-40

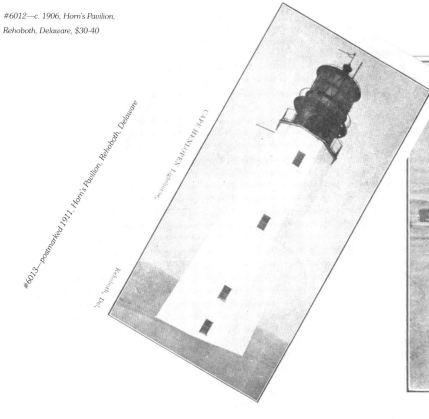

#6013--postmarked 1911, Horn's Pavilion, Rehoboth, Delaware

CAPE HENLOPEN LIGHTHOUSE

Rehoboth, Del.

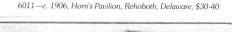

LONESOME   REHOBOTH, DEL.

No. 111.　　　The Life Saving Station, Rehoboth, Del.

Life Saving Station—No. 111

#6014—c. 1906, Horn's Pavilion, Rehoboth, Delaware, $60 (left)

The Wreck (of the Falmouth).

#6015—postmarked 1906, Horn's Pavilion, Rehoboth, Delaware, $50+

Launching the Life Boat—No. 113

#6016—c. 1906, Horn's Pavilion, Rehoboth, Delaware, $60+

Back from the Wreck

#6017—postmarked 1907, Horn's Pavilion, Rehoboth, Delaware, $40-50

The Breeches Buoy—Bringing a Sailor Ashore from a Shipwreck.

#6018—postmarked 1907, Horn's Pavilion, Rehoboth, Delaware, $60+

7 · BACK · FROM · THE · WRECK

Marion received your letter last night going home Saturday CCH.

THE WRECK, REHOBOTH, DEL.

THE BREECHES BUOY, REHOBOTH, DEL
BRINGING A SAILOR ASHORE FROM A SHIPWRECK

The Wonderful Sand Dune at Cape Henlopen—8 miles long, 150 feet high, 1 mile wide, covering a pine forest—Nothing but pure, clean, shifting sand, cast up by the winds.

#6019—c. 1906, Horn's Pavilion, Rehoboth, Delaware, $60+

THE WONDERFUL SAND DUNE AT CAPE HENLOPEN, REHOBOTH, DEL.
8 MILES LONG, 150 FEET HIGH, 1 MILE WIDE, COVERING A PINE FOREST. NOTHING BUT PURE, CLEAN,
SHIFTING SAND, CAST UP BY THE WINDS.

M.V. to F.V. Kenton Sept 1908

A SAFE BEACH,   Rehoboth, Del.

THE BOARDWALK NORTH FROM HORN'S

REHOBOTH, DEL.

NO. 198.   INTERIOR EPISCOPAL CHURCH.

FUN IN THE SURF, REHOBOTH, DEL.

ALL SAINTS' CHURCH REHOBOTH DEL.

Horn's Pavilion, Rehoboth Beach, Del.

#6026—postmarked 1911, Louis Kaufmann & Sons, Baltimore, Md., $50+

Boardwalk South from Horn's, Rehoboth Beach, Del.

#6028—postmarked 1912, Horn's, Rehoboth, Del., $30-35

1912 message to Miss Nellie,

"I have been down here resting up and trying to get fit by bathing in the briny sea. I have met quite a few friendly people and am having a very pleasant vacation."

#6027—postmarked 1910, Horn's, Rehoboth, Del., $25-30

#6029—postmarked 1910, Horn's-on-the-Boardwalk, Rehoboth Beach, Del., $30-40

Boardwalk North from Horn's, Rehoboth Beach, Del.

Coming from the Train, Rehoboth Beach, Del.

Horn's Royal Rink and Motion Picture Theatre, Rehoboth Beach, Del.

6032—postmarked 1911, Horn's, Rehoboth Beach, Del., $30-40

Royal Roller Skating Rink,
Rehoboth Beach, Del.

ROYAL ROLLER RINK

#6030—postmarked 1913, Louis Kaufmann & Sons, Baltimore, Md., $50+

Demonstrating the racial insensitivity sometimes found in turn of the century postcards, A Flock of Blackbirds—No. 102—shows us that ADORABLE is not a color- specific term. These cute kids find themselves on one of the more rare Horn's Pavilion cards.

#6025—postmarked 1906, Horn's Pavilion, Rehoboth, Delaware, $60+

o. 102.

A FLOCK OF BLACK BIRDS.
REHOBOTH, DEL.

1910 message to Charles,

"We are enjoying the ocean breezes. The wind has been blowing a gale and the waves dashing high, but we enjoy the bathing none the less. Best Regards"

A Trolley Ride, Rehoboth, Del.

GO SLOW
SPEED NOT TO EXCEED
12 MILES AN HOUR
UNDER ORDER OF MAYOR

#6031—c. 1910, Louis Kaufmann & Sons, Baltimore, Md., $40-50

Having a High Old Time in the Surf at
Rehoboth Beach, Del.

#6033—postmarked 1923, Louis Kaufmann & Sons, Baltimore, Md., $10-15

The Old Oaken Bucket, Rehoboth Beach, Del.

#6035—postmarked 1915, Horn's-on-the-Boardwalk, Rehoboth Beach, Del., $15-20

St. Agnes Catholic Church.

St. Agnes by the Sea Sisters Home,
Rehoboth Beach, Del.

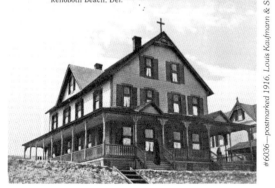

#6036—postmarked 1916, Louis Kaufmann & Sons, Baltimore, Md., $15-20

#6034—c. 1910, Louis Kaufmann & Sons, Baltimore, Md., $20-25

1928 message to Helen,

"Down here having a fine time.
Gained 11 lbs and sunburned.
Yours, Jim"

Brayton Hotel, Rehoboth Beach, Del.

THE PUBLIC SCHOOL. Rehoboth Beach, Del.

THE CLUB HOUSE Rehoboth Beach, Del.

VIEWS OF REHOBOTH, DEL.

#6038—postmarked 1906, Horn's Pavilion, Rehoboth, Delaware, $25-30

Waiting for Summer Time, Rehoboth Beach, Del.

#6039—c. 1910, Horn's-on-the-Boardwalk, $40-50

#6042—postmarked 1902, publisher unknown, $40-50

REHOBOTH AVENUE - South Side

1907 message to My Dear Laura,

"Have just had a fine ocean bath and at 1:30 PM Mr. Douglas, Tom and I leave for Lewes, Del. to fish this afternoon. Tomorrow morning Mr. Douglas and I go out on ocean with some fisherman to get some fish and at 1:30 tomorrow we leave for house. Am having a fine time and feeling well. Lovingly, Dave"

#6041—postmarked 1914, Horn's-on-the-Boardwalk, $20-25

#6040—c. 1910, Horn's-on-the-Boardwalk, $40-50

The Bathing Beach, Rehoboth Beach, Del.

The Turn of the Tide, Rehoboth Beach, Del.

FENNA. NOON TRAIN, REHOBOTH, DEL.

Pub. by W. J. Ruddell

#6043—c. 1908, W. J. Ruddell, $100+

ANNUAL ENCAMPMENT, REHOBOTH, DEL.

Pub. by Geo. W. Rafferty

#6045-postmarked 1908, Geo. W. Rafferty, $60+

#6044—postmarked 1908, Geo. W. Rafferty, $75+

1911 message to Mrs. Franklin,

"Assure Momma that I am still alive. I was in this morning as soon as the excursion train came in."

#6046—postmarked 1908, Geo. W. Rafferty, $40-50

SOLDIERS ON MARCH FROM TRAIN, REHOBOTH, DEL.

Pub. by Geo. W. Rafferty

REHOBOTH, DEL.

REHOBOTH'S RAPID TRANSIT.

Pub. by Geo. W. Rafferty

Many thanks for candy.

45

BIRDS EYE VIEW OF REHOBOTH Del.   J. T. Waples.

#6047—c. 1908, J. T. Waples, $40-50

PILOT BOAT, REHOBOTH, DEL.   Pub. by Geo. W. Rafferty

#6048—c. 1908, Geo. W. Rafferty, $20-25

Handwritten note on reverse of local interest:

"A very well known picture of the Railroad Station. Some local people standing on the platform include Lester Johnson, Elmer Button, Joseph Lynch, Gertna Joseph."

A STATION SCENE, REHOBOTH BEACH, DEL.

#6049—c. 1918, Louis Kaufmann & Sons, Baltimore, Md., $40-50

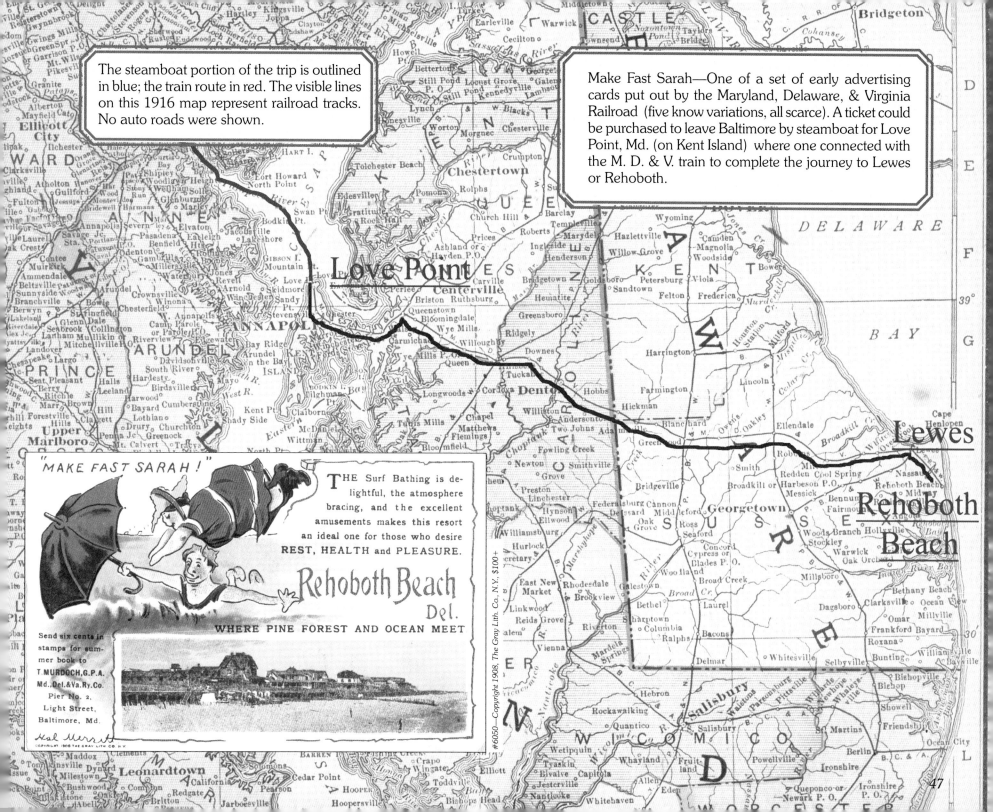

The steamboat portion of the trip is outlined in blue; the train route in red. The visible lines on this 1916 map represent railroad tracks. No auto roads were shown.

Make Fast Sarah—One of a set of early advertising cards put out by the Maryland, Delaware, & Virginia Railroad (five know variations, all scarce). A ticket could be purchased to leave Baltimore by steamboat for Love Point, Md. (on Kent Island) where one connected with the M. D. & V. train to complete the journey to Lewes or Rehoboth.

"MAKE FAST SARAH!"

THE Surf Bathing is delightful, the atmosphere bracing, and the excellent amusements makes this resort an ideal one for those who desire REST, HEALTH and PLEASURE.

Rehoboth Beach
Del.

WHERE PINE FOREST AND OCEAN MEET

Send six cents in stamps for summer book to T. MURDOCH, G.P.A. Md., Del. & Va. Ry. Co. Pier No. 2, Light Street, Baltimore, Md.

#6050—Copyright 1908, The Gray Lith. Co., N.Y., $100+

U. S. LIFE SAVING STATION, REHOBOTH BEACH, DEL.

#6051—postmarked 1916, Louis Kaufmann & Sons, Baltimore, Md., $40-50

#6052—CT production code 1925, Louis Kaufmann & Sons, Baltimore, Md., $10-15

#6053—c. 1920, Horn's, Inc., Rehoboth Beach, Del., $30-35

Parking on Rehoboth Ave … you thought parking problems were something new?

#6054—CT production code 1928, Louis Kaufmann & Sons, Baltimore, Md., $20-25

CANOEING ON SILVER LAKE. REHOBOTH BEACH. DELAWARE.

106231

SOUTH SIDE OF REHOBOTH AVENUE FROM CARLTON HOTEL. REHOBOTH BEACH. DEL

12267

SOUTH SIDE OF REHOBOTH AVENUE, LOOKING TOWARDS BEACH, REHOBOTH BEACH, DELAWARE.

#6055—CT production code 1925, Louis Kaufmann & Sons, Ba ltimore, Md., $30-35

#6055a—c. 1920, Horn's, Inc., Rehoboth Beach, Del., $15-20

REHOBOTH AVENUE AND THE ATLANTIC OCEAN, REHOBOTH BEACH. DEL.

1929 message to Walter,

"You ought to try out your new car on some of these roads and come down some weekend. I'm sure you and Elsie would like it here. Always, Addison"

#6056—c. 1925, Louis Kaufmann & Sons, Baltimore, Md., $8-10

THE OLD OAKEN BUCKET AND HOMESTEAD, REHOBOTH BEACH, DEL.

#6057—postmarked 1932, Louis Kaufmann & Sons, Baltimore, Md., $15-20

BOARD WALK AND BEACH LOOKING NORTH REHOBOTH BEACH DEL

SOUTH END OF BOARD WALK AND PLAYLAND, REHOBOTH BEACH, DEL.

#6060—postmarked 1934, Louis Kaufmann & Sons, Baltimore, Md., $10-15

BEACH AND BOARDWALK LOOKING NORTH FROM FISHING PIER, REHOBOTH BEACH, DEL.

1934 message to Anne,

"You ought to be here with us. There is plenty of excitement. The other evening a man in his plane crashed right into the ocean! He was killed. You should have seen him and his plane when it was dragged into shore. Love, Catherine"

#6058—CT production code 1928, Louis Kaufmann & Sons, Baltimore, Md., $8-10

#6061—CT production code 1930, Louis Kaufmann & Sons, Baltimore, Md., $20-25

#6059—CT production code 1925, Louis Kaufmann & Sons, Baltimore, Md., $10-15

MINIATURE GOLF COURSE SHOWING METHODIST CHURCH, REHOBOTH BEACH, DEL.

BOARD WALK AND PIER, LOOKING SOUTH, REHOBOTH BEACH, DELAWARE

BELHAVEN HOTEL, REHOBOTH BEACH, DEL.

122683

#6062—CT production code 1928, Louis Kaufmann & Sons, Baltimore, Md., $8-10

1947 message to Gilbert,

"Well here we are at Rehoboth, staying at the Belhaven Hotel, sports for a day. It is an awful lot. Love, Gram"

#6063—CT production code 1925, Louis Kaufmann & Sons, Baltimore, Md., $10-15

#6065—CT production code 1914, Louis Kaufmann & Sons, Baltimore, Md., $10-15

HENLOPEN HOTEL, REHOBOTH BEACH, DEL.

1930 message to John,

"Having a fine time. Lots of fried chicken and water melon. Today we are having a big goose. Going to the factory and see them make catsup this morning. Nellie & all"

#6064—postmarked 1938, Louis Kaufmann & Sons, Baltimore, Md., $8-10

HOTEL CARLTON, REHOBOTH BEACH, DELAWARE.

Hotel Carlton before new façade.

106229

Hotel Carlton after new façade.

59 HOTEL CARLTON, REHOBOTH BEACH, DEL.

122674

HENLOPEN HOTEL AND BOARD WALK, REHOBOTH BEACH, DEL.

#6066—CT production code 1916, Louis Kaufmann & Sons, Baltimore, Md., $8-10

#6067—postmarked 1930, Louis Kaufmann & Sons, Baltimore, Md., $10-15

1938 message to Lillian,

"Everything here is lovely and all are well. The private beach is stoneless—lovely, clean, white sand and surf bathing. The wild flowers and birds are different and interesting. Drives and boardwalk prove delightful. Love from all, Helen"

#6068—CT production code 1914, Louis Kaufmann & Sons, Baltimore, Md., $10-12

#6069—CT production code 1916, Louis Kaufmann & Sons, Baltimore, Md., $8-10

OLIVE AVENUE, SHOWING EPISCOPAL CHURCH, REHOBOTH BEACH, DEL.

SAINT AGNES-BY-THE-SEA, REHOBOTH BEACH, DEL.

REHOBOTH BEACH COUNTRY CLUB, REHOBOTH BEACH, DEL.

#6070—c. 1920, Horn's, Inc., Rehoboth Beach, Del., $10-15

PARK AVENUE, LOOKING TOWARDS OCEAN, REHOBOTH BEACH, DELAWARE.

1932 message to Mrs. Wade,

"arrived all right. We drove for five hours. Weather is hot as the devil. Hope it gets hotter. Matt"

#6073—postmarked 1928, Louis Kaufmann & Sons, Baltimore, Md., $10-15

#6072—CT production code 1928, Harry P. Cann & Bros., Baltimore, Md., $10-15

#6071—CT production code 1928, Louis Kaufmann & Sons, Baltimore, Md., $10-15

Bridge across Silver Lake, Rehoboth Beach, Del.

COUNTRY CLUB, REHOBOTH BEACH, DEL.

122676

#6078—CT production code 1928, Louis Kaufmann & Sons, Baltimore, Md., $10-15

122667

#6080—CT production code 1928, Louis Kaufmann & Sons, Baltimore, Md., $10-12

1926 message to Ruth, (on car among the pines card)

"The cottage is made from a discarded railroad car and is attractive as can be. We go bathing every day and enjoy every minute. Love, Towny"

1952 message to Charles,

"Have been eating clams, crabs, fish, and blueberries. Be seeing you and don't work too hard. Frank & Martha"

#6081—CT production code 1914, Louis Kaufmann & Sons, Baltimore, Md., $10-15

#6079—postmarked 1915, Louis Kaufmann & Sons, Baltimore, Md., $10-12

THE R. R. COACH AMONG THE PINES, REHOBOTH BEACH, DEL.

BUNGALOWS AT CORNER OF SURF AND COLUMBIA AVENUE, REHOBOTH BEACH, DEL.

#6082—postmarked 1929, Louis Kaufmann & Sons, Baltimore, Md., $10-15

1940 message,

"Dear Grace, I hope that you and Jesse and Daisy will consider this card to you all. It is the picture of the beautiful drive through the pines, which terminates at the ocean. Swimming here is wonderful—so warm—especially this past two weeks. I have had a grand time with my two wards. Both swell kids. Love, Jay"

1910 message to Mrs. Evans,

"Dear Aunt, The doctor ordered milk for me so I walk through the pines every morning to go to the farm house after the milk. It is a beautiful place. It is nothing but pine trees. Your loving niece, Lottie"

#6084—c. 1920, Horn's, Inc., Rehoboth Beach, Del., $15-20

#6083—CT production code 1914, Louis Kaufmann & Sons, Baltimore, Md., $6-8

HOMES IN THE PINES, REHOBOTH BEACH, DEL.

COLUMBIA AVENUE AMONG THE PINES, REHOBOTH BEACH, DEL.

RHUMBA TEA DANSANT AT THE BEACH CLUB

#6085—postmarked 1941, The Collotype Co., Elizabeth, N.J., Hand Colored, $50+

Printed ad from reverse of Rhumba Tea Dansant.

1941 message to Grace,

"Here I am … Some troubadour singing to the moon almost every night and in every song there goes a thought for you."

A Cabana Party—Indian Beach Club.

#6086—postmarked 1941, The Collotype Co., Elizabeth, N.J., $10-15

#6087—c. 1940, The Mayrose Co., Linden, N.J., $6-8

A CABANA PARTY

ENTRANCE TO REHOBOTH BEACH, DEL

CARLTON HOTEL, REHOBOTH BEACH, DEL.

#6088—c. 1940, L. H. Roth, Rehoboth Beach, Del., $8-10

BOARDWALK, REHOBOTH BEACH, DEL.

#6090—c. 1940, The Mayrose Co., Linden, N.J., $10-12

#6089—c. 1940, The Mayrose Co., Linden, N.J., $8-10

SCENE OF BOARDWALK AND BEACH, REHOBOTH BEACH, DEL.

1958 message,

"Dear Aunt Edna, We're all having lots of fun. The waves are huge and Dean just loves it but it's really kind of rough for me. The children are having lots of good times. They even went crabbing along the edge of the canal this morning. Love Dean, Jeanne, Sally & Susan"

1937 message to Marian,

"This ocean breeze is doing things to me. Sara"

REHOBOTH BEACH, DEL.

Edwards Treasure Chest —

#6091—c. 1940, L. H. Roth, Rehoboth Beach, Del., $10-12

1959 message to "The Force"
c/o Wilmington Savings Fund Society,

*"Weather hot and water wonderful. Am doing a
lot of nothing and enjoying it very much."*

1950 message to Miss Gerry,
c/o Bell Telephone Co. Sorting Unit,
2nd floor, Pittsburgh

*"Dear Gerry, arrived safe and sound Sat.
evening. The place sure is beautiful. I sent
3 lbs salt water taffy for the girls of the unit.
I hope you get it before I get back. I hate to
say it but I'll be seeing you soon. Lil"*

#6092—c. 1940, The Mayrose Co., Linden, N.J., $6-8

NORTH EAST STORM AT REHOBOTH BEACH, DEL.

#6093—c. 1940, Collotype Co., Elizabeth, N.J., $10-15

16 Delaware Ave.

SURF BATHING - FISHING - SAILING
Beach umbrellas furnished Guests
(In Rehoboth turn right at First Street
traffic light, two blocks turn left on
Delaware or three blocks turn left on
Brooklyn.)
TRAVEL BY BUS
For daily schedule to Rehoboth consult:
Red Star Motor Coach - Baltimore
Greyhound Bus Lines - Washington
Short Line - Wilmington and Philadelphia

ENGEL HALL
Rehoboth Beach, Del. Phone Reh. 2501
Attractive, home-like stopping places
situated in the ocean block. Convenient
to beach and boardwalk.
Hot and Cold Baths - Free Parking

14 Brooklyn Ave.

#6094—c. 1940, L. H. Roth, Rehoboth Beach, Del., $10-12

SHAW PARK TRAILER CAMP, REHOBOTH BEACH, DEL.

#6096—postmarked 1939, L. H. Roth, Rehoboth Beach, Del., $10-12

1953 message,

"Dear Jane, I've been having a very relaxing time here for the past week. Wish this life of ocean bathing, swimming, clam-digging, boat rides, etc. could go on longer! As Ever, Dot"

#6097—postmarked 1939, L. H. Roth, Rehoboth Beach, Del., $8-10

#6095—c. 1940, The Mayrose Co., Linden, N.J., $10-12

LAKE DRIVE, REHOBOTH BEACH, DEL.

SHAW PARK TRAILER CAMP, REHOBOTH BEACH, DEL.

#6098—postmarked 1956, Tichnor Bros., Boston, Mass., $6-8

1951 message to Edna,

"Spent Sat. P.M. & evening at this beach. It was so refreshing and exhilarating to be at the ocean once again. We have had some hot weather. Came for a wedding and it was lovely. Marjorie"

1948 message to Mr. & Mrs. Finney,

"Hi Folks, The lazy life is about to ruin me. The weather has been nice so far and the food wonderful. I'm going to hate to start back to work Mon. V. Ingall"

JUST THE RIGHT TEMPERATURE S-319

#6099—CT production code 1934, Curteich-Chicago, $10-15

GREETINGS FROM REHOBOTH BEACH, DEL. 4A-H1228

#6103—postmarked 1942, Edwards Stores, Inc., $4-6

Hotel Plaza, Rehoboth Beach, Del.

#6101—c. 1950, C. H. Ruth, Washington, D.C., $10-12

Hotel Carlton and Rehoboth Trust Co., Rehoboth Beach, Del.

#6100—c. 1950, Rehoboth 5 cent to $1 Store, Rehoboth Beach, Del., $8-10

1956 message,

"Dear Betty, If you have a formula for holding back time please send me a wire. I've never seen time go by so fast. Needless to say we're having a perfectly marvelous vacation. Love, Dottie"

#6102—CT production code 1944, Harry P. Cann & Bros., Baltimore, Md., $6-8

4B-H1324

#6104—postmarked 1947, Edwards Stores, Inc., $6-8

1949 message to Mrs. Woodward,

"We're having a fine vacation here. The beach is all you & Lewis said it was. Swimming and sunning & eating & sleeping & some running is our schedule each day. See you next week. Love Allen"

#6105—c. 1945, Tichnor Bros., Boston, Mass., $4-6

#6106—CT production code 1944, Harry P. Cann & Bros., Baltimore, Md., $6-8

17—Hotel Carlton, Rehoboth Beach, Delaware

1945 message to Mr. & Mrs. Kirk,

"Weather has been excellent here since we've been down. Wish you could be here to enjoy it with us. Steve is catching lots of fish. Caught a seven pound black bass yesterday. Lucille is fine and putting on a few extra pounds. Hope Earl is feeling better. Now that the war is over perhaps his job will be lighter for a while. See you after Labor Day. Don"

#6107—CT production code 1947, Harry P. Cann & Bros., Baltimore, Md., $6-8

North meeting South, where anything can happen.
Rehoboth Beach, Delaware

#6109—c. 1945, Tichnor Bros., Boston, Mass., $8-10

7 — Boardwalk Scene
Rehoboth Beach, Delaware

*Dill's Salt Water Taffy &
Popcorn and Bayberry Gift Shop.*

1950 message to Sue Ann,

"Am having a good time. I was fishing and crabbing. Beside that I just eat and sleep. I am real lazy. Grammy"

#6108—CT production code 1953, Harry P. Cann & Bros., Baltimore, Md., $6-8

#6110—CT production code 1940, Harry P. Cann & Bros., Baltimore, Md., $4-6

#6111—c. 1950, C. H. Ruth, Washington, D.C., $10-15

Stokes Inn — Rehoboth Beach, Del.

Hotel Lobby   Dining Room

31—Replica of Henlopen Lighthouse at Night,
Rehoboth Beach, Del.

REPLICA
Henlopen Lighthouse
Built 1725
Rebuilt by Merchants
of Philadelphia
and Delaware
1764
Destroyed by Storms
April 13, 1926

Henlopen Hotel, Rehoboth Beach, Delaware

#6112—c. 1945, Tichnor Bros., Boston, Mass., $10-12

1950 message to Esther,

"We are enjoying our-selves very much. It is cloudy today, so we are renting bikes. We talked on telephone yesterday to Wilmington. and were surprised to hear that it was pouring rain."

#6113—c. 1945, Tichnor Bros., Boston, Mass., $10-12

ABBEY COTTAGE
Cor. 1st St. and Maryland Ave.
Rehoboth Beach, Delaware

#6114—c. 1945, Tichnor Bros., Boston, Mass., $8-10

Summer Home of Mrs. Rodney Sharp, Rehoboth Beach, Del.

Scene Showing Wreck of an Oil Tanker Driven Ashore   20

During Tropical Hurricane, Autumn, 1944, Rehoboth, Del.   75344

#6115—dated 1944, Del Mar News Agency, Wilmington, Del., $15-20

THE MARY ANN INN
MARY A. SULLIVAN
OLIVE AVENUE,   REHOBOTH BEACH, DEL.
HOME COOKING — FAMILY SERVICE

#6116—c. 1940, publisher unknown, $6-8

The Mary Ann Inn (business card).

#6117—c. 1955, Geiger Bros., Newark, N.J., $8-10

Ad on business card reverse.

BEVIS COTTAGE, 15 HICKMAN ST., REHOBOTH, DELAWARE   D-221

Bevis Cottage, 15 Hickman St., Ocean Block, Comfortable Rooms with private or semi-private baths. Outside enclosed hot showers for your convenience when returning from the beach. Owned and operated by Mr. and Mrs. Wm. W. Bevis.

BODDY'S HOTEL—REHOBOTH BEACH. DEL.

ROOMS WITH RUNNING WATER   FAMOUS FOR FOODS AND LOW RATES

C 572

#6118—postmarked 1941, Fort Wayne Printing Co., Fort Wayne, Ind., $10-12

1947 message,

"Hello Phyllis, You should see the frozen custard here but not as nice as Washington. Emma"

1 MILE SOUTH OF REHOBOTH BEACH. DEL. ROUTE 14

D-160

#6119—c. 1955, Geiger Bros., Newark, N.J., $10-12

#6120—c. 1955, National Press, Inc., North Chicago, $15-20

1949 message,

"Dear Ann, I am having a swell time. Rehoboth is a nice place. I've learned to do the back bend but not good. Well good-by. Love, Jerry"

AVE, REST COCKTAIL LOUNGE - Rehoboth Ave. - Rehoboth Beach - Phone 8863 - 8944

Rehoboth Beach as You Remember It

#6121—c. 1958, Rodgers Record and Photo Shop, Rehoboth Beach, Delaware, $6-8

Rehoboth Avenue—50s Cars.

#6124—postmarked 1962, Snyder & Rodgers, Rehoboth Beach, Del., Color by C. H. Ruth, $5-6

Boardwalk showing Dolle's.

#6122—c. 1955, Rodgers Record and Photo Shop, Rehoboth Beach, Delaware, $6-8

Rehoboth Avenue.

1970 message,

"Dear Amy, Some friends of Jo's brought me here for a rest. Am sitting looking out at the ocean. Warm in the sun. Not too many in swimming as it's quite rough. I'm enjoying the sun and sleeping.
Love, Edith"

#6123—c. 1960, Photo-Lite Camera Shop, Salisbury, Maryland, $6-8

1956 message to Mom and Dad and Buck,

"I am getting a pretty nice tan. Tomorrow I am going to put 'Light and Bright' on my hair. I hope it turns out ok. Sharon"

Sun View Motel.

#6124a – c.1960, Dexter Press, West Nyack, N. Y., Color by J. Paul Rodgers, $6-8

1960s message,

"Dear Aunt Sis & Uncle Harvey, We sure have had fun! So far we went to Ocean City & Rehoboth Boardwalk. We got sausages and sandwiches made of candy that really look real. They taste delicious. Dad has bleached his hair. Love, Mildred"

Welcome Shriners.

Welcome Shriners

#6125—c. 1965, Snyder & Rodgers, Rehoboth Beach, Delaware., Color by J. Paul Rodgers, $8-10

Rehoboth Beach Volunteer Fire Company.

1948 message to Mr. & Mrs. Kirk,

"Well the season here is almost over and it won't be long now. Sept. is a nice month at the Shore but you never know what to expect next. Hear you have or had quite a garden. Practice up on 500 [rummy] if you don't want to get a good licking this winter. Don"

Room rate chart from reverse.

#6127—postmarked 1963, Snyder & Rodgers, Rehoboth Beach, Del., $8-10

Jack Dentino's Amusement Center.

#6126—c. 1965, Tingle Printing Co., Pittsville, Md., $5-6

#6129—c. 1960, Tingle Printing Co.,
Colourpicture, Boston, Mass., $6-8

1970 message,

"Dear Mom & Leroy, The weather has been lovely, the beach is fun, our beach house is very pleasant & we get along very well with our friends who came with us. However, I stupidly!! went into the water with my glasses on & lost them in a big wave, so today we have been running around trying to replace them. Love, Bev, Bob, and the boys"

#6128—postmarked 1967, Tingle Printing Co., Pittsville, Md., Color by F. W. Brueckmann, $6-8

Rehoboth Beach Surfers.

Bethany, Dewey, Indian River Inlet, and Fenwick Island

Bethany

1921 message to Miss Dorothy,

"This picture was taken in the year one. Reminds me of the one you sent me illustrated with the octogenarian piscatorial artists."

Hotel Townsend—building on right has a sign for Long's (Bath House?) with prices for changing and lockers.

The Bus, Bethany Beach, Del.

#7001—postmarked 1921, publisher unknown, $50+

#7003—postmarked 1935, real photo, processor unknown, $60+

Hotel Townsend

#7002—postmarked 1909, publisher unknown, $35-45

SEASIDE INN, BETHANY BEACH, DEL.

GEORGE H. & MARY FOUSE THOWNSEND, PROPS.

#7004—postmarked 1929, publisher unknown, $35-45

West Breeze Hotel—the porch railing has two clusters of small American flags flapping in the breeze.

West Breeze Hotel   Bethany Beach, Delaware

#7006—c. 1940, for H. A. Frazer, Bethany Beach, Del., by The Albertype Co., Brooklyn, N.Y., $20-25

1936 message to Lee,

"Just arrived in camp, have a fine time, will send letter on Friday, Love & Kisses, Joc … I need $ Bad"

1942 message to Miss Diver,

"Every thing is just grand in June. Am well satisfied & feeling fine. This salt air has sure put wind in my sails. Been in two times two days & sleep on beach all afternoon. Sykes have made several improvements in place and it is attractive and comfortable. Love, Drew"

213th C. A. (A-a) P. National Guard en route to Annual Encampment.

1910 message to Emily,

"This is where Martin is at camp. It's a nice place and the bathing is great. Betty"

#7005—c. 1910, postmarked from Bethany Beach, Del., year not legible, Dalrymple Print, Easton, Pa., $30-35

BETHANY BEACH, DELAWARE

#7007—c. 1940, for H. A. Frazer, Bethany Beach, Del., by The Albertype Co., Brooklyn, N.Y., $15-20

1935 message to William,

"Maude and I are down here in Bethany. Having a wonderful time. Go in bathing every day. Wish you were here. Ma"

The place in the foreground is Ringler's at Bethany Beach. This happened in the recent storm we had.

72

#7009—c. 1940, $15-20

GUESS WE WON'T BE ABLE TO DANCE HERE EVER AGAIN

Ringler's at Bethany, an old photograph with a sad story to tell.

Inlet Bridge—1941.

INLET BRIDGE NEAR BETHANY BEACH, DELAWARE

#7010—postmarked 1941, for H. A. Frazer, Bethany Beach, Del., by The Albertype Co., Brooklyn, N.Y., $15-20

ADDY-SEA   BETHANY BEACH, DELAWARE

#7011—postmarked 1955, The Albertype Co., Brooklyn, N.Y., $15-20

#7008-c. 1940, for H.A. Frazer, Bethany Beach, Del., by The AlbertypeCo., Brooklyn, N.Y., $15-20

*Bethany Breakers Apartments—
Mrs. Ada L. Hildenbrand, Owner-Manager.*

#7012—postmarked 1954, Curteich-Chicago, $10-15

Warren's Restaurant   Bethany Beach, Delaware

BETHANY BREAKERS APARTMENTS — BETHANY BEACH, DELAWARE

Endless Boardwalk.

#7013—postmarked 1954, Tichnor Bros., Boston, Mass., $8-10

Boardwalk, Bethany Beach, Delaware

76342

1936 message to Mrs. Perkins,

"It is lovely here but the nights have been cold. Full moon last night, beautiful."

Fabulous 50s view looking east toward the ocean.

Nomad Village Motor Lodge & Efficiencies – Package store – Cocktail lounge – private pool & beach.

Professional photographer Nick Varrato still operates NaVar Studios in Millsboro, Del. When I called about using the card, Nick recollected this early 60s aerial shot and the camera he used to create it some 40 years ago.

#7014—c. 1955, Tichnor Bros., Boston, Mass., $8-10

#7015- Postmarked 1966, NaVar Studio, Millsboro, Delaware, $5-6

Boardwalk at Bethany.

#7015a—postmarked 1965, Mardelva News Co., Salisbury, Md, $4-5

Dewey

Oceanside. *Bayside.*

GREETINGS FROM DEWEY BEACH, DELAWARE

#7017—c. 1960, Color by C. H. Ruth, Snyder & Rodgers, Rehoboth Beach, Del., $5-6

Greetings from Dewey Beach, Del.

#7016—c. 1960, Tingle Printing Co., Pittsville, Md., $5-6

Dewey Beach looking south—"Frank Denmeads famous 'Redwood Lodge' and "Southwinds Motel' can be seen in the center."

Harry Shaud's Bottle and Cork Bar—Cocktail Lounge—Liquor Store—Live Entertainment—Dancing every night.

#7017a—postmarked 1957, Color by C. H. Ruth, Rodgers Record & Photo Shop, Rehoboth Beach, Del., $5-6

#7018—c. 1960, Hannau Color Productions, Miami Beach, Fla., $5-6

Indian River Inlet

The Boat House on Rehoboth Bay at Dewey Beach – Ownership/Management – Mr. & Mrs. C. Pearce Cody. Telephone: Rehoboth 8868

Massey Landing, Delaware's Popular Fishing, Clamming and Boating Resort, Located Between Rehoboth & Indian River Bays.

#7019—postmarked 1958, real photo, processor unknown, $25-30

#7019b – c. 1965, Color by J. Paul Rodgers, Snyder & Rodgers, Rehoboth Beach, Del., $6-8

#7018a – hand dated 1958, John V. Pontiere, Jr., Ocean City, N. J., $8-10

Note from Virginia, Cecil, and Mother,

"Had dinner here Saturday Aug. 9th, 1958. Sold in Spring 1961, now called Cap'n Hank's Boat House Restaurant & Cocktail Lounge"

Riding the Surf—A Sport of Kings.

1968 message to Rick,

Right now we are sitting here watching these fellows surfing. They are really good. There is about 30 of them in. Having a good time. Miss you. Love, Mom & Dad"

#7019a—postmarked 1968, Snyder & Rodgers, Rehoboth Beach, Delaware, $6-8

Fenwick Island

#7020—c. 1965, Color photo by F. W. Brueckmann, Tingle Printing Co., Pittsville, Md., $7-8

1952 message,

"Dear Yvonne, I am having a wonderful time at Fenwick Island. Yesterday we went away out in the ocean. I haven't had too much sunburn but am turning brown. Wish you were here. Love, Sara"

#7020a—postmarked 1959, Color by C. H. Ruth, Rodgers Record & Photo Shop, Rehoboth Beach, Del., $5-6

1965 message,

"Weather is just delightful now. We crabbed successfully today and hope the fishing tomorrow will be good. If not, hamburger! Jane B"

E. B. McCabe General Store—(phone)
Tel. Georgetown, Del.
Ex. Dickinson 488.
Fenwich Island, Del.

#7021—c. 1955, S & T Photo Service, Milford, Del., $25-30

1953 message to Lawrence (from child to another child),

"Dear Larry, I am having a fine time in Fenwick Island. I have gone in swimming every day so far. It has been real hot here. Good-by for now, Your pal, Francis"

1955 message to Zitta (from a child),

"Dear Moma, Wish you would come down this week-end. Today we were out swimming and we found a lot of conch shells. We had about twenty or twenty five. P.S. Don't forget to come down this week-end."

#7022—CT production date 1951, Harry P. Cann & Bros., Baltimore, Md., $8-10

Postmark faint, but appears to be 1953, message to Mrs. Gordon,

"Decided to stay another week. Have experienced my first hurricane. State police got us out at 3:30 AM Friday. Drove to mainland & spent day in a church. Caught my first four fish today. The water is wonderful and I'm beginning to feel like a human being. Katherine"

Interior of Lighthouse Diner.

#7024—c. 1960, John V. Pontiere, Jr., Ocean City, N.J., $8-10

#7023—c. 1960, John V. Pontiere, Jr., Ocean City, N. J. $8-10

The Lighthouse Diner—Ownership/ Management—Madison Gray.

Ocean City

The Pier Entrance, Ocean City, Md.

#8001—c. 1910, Louis Kaufmann & Sons, Baltimore, Md., $20-25

1962 message to Mr. & Mrs. Brosch,

"All is well. Weather is ideal so far. Had a bon fire on beach & swam at inlet till 11 last night. Gary caught 12 blue fish today on rocks. Alma & Jim just left to go crabbing over in bay. Love, Bert & Walt"

#8002—postmarked 1916, Louis Kaufmann & Sons, Baltimore, Md., $40-50

Scene on Boardwalk, Ocean City, Md.

1909 message to Ginger,

"If Virginia could only see me now!!! Seated in Mr. Messick's tent at Ocean City. Being royally entertained and taking excellent care of him. You can imagine what life in a tent at the seashore is with such visitors. I could stay here forever. J. F."

#8003—CT production code 1913, Louis Kaufmann & Sons, Baltimore, Md., $15-20

#8004—postmarked 1917, The Chessler Co., Baltimore, Md., $30-40

1908 message to Lena,

"This is a scene or view from the Eastern Shore. Don't think I have forgotten your rocks, rivulets, and rills, tho I now am listening to the ocean's roar. Come down."

#8005—postmarked 1909, Spetzler, Connor, & Coffin, Made in Germany, $15-20

1914 message to Kenny,

"If you were only here with Louis I know you would enjoy rolling the balls with him and playing on beach. Uncle Louis"

From Edna

ST. ROSE SUMMER HOME, OCEAN CITY, MD.

#8010—Copyright 1907 by Sudwarth Co., Washington, D.C., $15-20

Boardwalk showing Maryland Pharmacy.

Board Walk, Ocean City, Md.

Maryland Pharmacy.

#8012—c. 1910, Louis Kaufmann & Sons, Baltimore, Md., $10-15

No. 2060. Copyrighted 1906 by Franz Huld, Publisher, New York

A Wave Vision   Ocean City, Md.

Imagine yourself taking a dip. Love to my dear mama. Rosa Appler

#8011—Copyrighted 1906 by Franz Huld, New York, $30-40

1944 message to Mrs. Herrell,

"We have been down here since Sunday. Staying at a pleasant place with friendly people. Feeling better. Charlie and Connie"

U. S. Life Saving Station, Hand Colored.

#8014—postmarked 1914, for F. J. Harmonson, $40

U. S. Life Saving Station.

OCEAN CITY, Md.

U.S. LIFE SAVING STATION

Hand-Colored.

U. S. Life Saving Station, posing with baby.

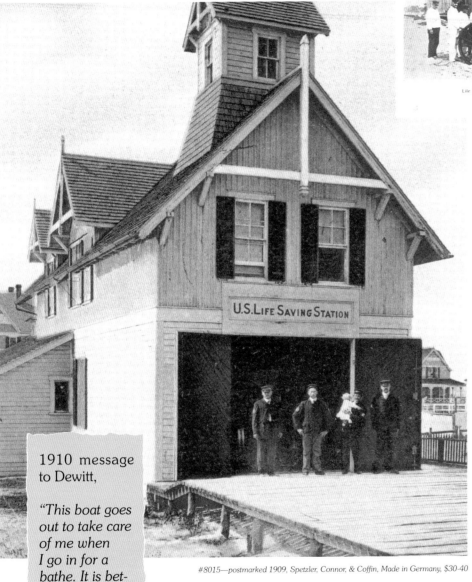

Life Savers Drilling, Ocean City, Md.

Aug 26th 1907
Uncle Polly & Nana

#8016—dated 1907, Washington Pharmacy, Ocean City, Md., $15-20

U. S. Life Saving Station, Ocean City, Md.

#8013—c. 1910, Louis Kaufmann & Sons, Baltimore, Md., $25-30

U. S. Life Savers, Ocean City, Md.

1909 message to Mr. Goetzman,

"Received your card OK. Are you still tired? The darkies had their concert last night—the one we went to. R. B."

#8018—c. 1910, publisher unknown, $10-15

1910 message to Dewitt,

"This boat goes out to take care of me when I go in for a bathe. It is better than strawberry jam or carmels. Della"

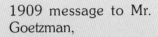

U.S. LIFE SAVING STATION

#8015—postmarked 1909, Spetzler, Connor, & Coffin, Made in Germany, $30-40

Bringing in the Life Boat   *At Ocean City, Md.*

86

Greetings from Ocean City.

MARYLAND

Maryland State Seal—8 View.

#8019—Copyrighted 1908 by Franz Huld Company, New York, $15-20

#8017—postmarked 1918, Louis Kaufmann & Sons, Baltimore, Md., $20-25

LIFE SAVING DRILL, U. S. LIFE SAVING STATION, OCEAN CITY, MD.

#8020—postmarked 1913, publisher unknown, $8-10

Atlantic Avenue.   OCEAN CITY, Md.

Hand-colored

#8019a—postmarked 1910, for Dr. F. J. Townsend, by The Albertype Co., Brooklyn, N.Y., $25-30

1945 message to Bud,

"Dear Bud, How are you. I am okay with a gallon of water in my stomach. I am having a lot of fun down here. The other day a big wave knocked me down and I scraped my nose. Well I guess I close because there is no more room to write. Your friend, Reggie"

1914 message to Miss Ida,

"Having lots to eat. The boat trip is best but train [is] dirty. Brother Paul"

OCEAN CITY, MD.

Lawd a massy! Dis am some swift town

#8021—Copyright 1913, S. Bergman, New York, $10-15

In the Good Old Summer Time on the Beach.

#8022—c. 1910, publisher unknown, $6-8

SHOWELL'S SWIMMING POOL, OCEAN CITY, MD.

#8023—c. 1920, Louis Kaufmann & Sons, Baltimore, Md., $15-20

#8025—postmarked 1915, The Chessler Co., Baltimore, Md., $50+B

#8024—postmarked 1908, Spetzler, Connor, & Coffin, Made in Germany, $75+

TRAIN CROSSING SYNEPUXENT BAY, OCEAN CITY, MD.

#8029 c. 1910, Louis Kaufmann & Sons, Baltimore, Md., $20-25

#8027—postmarked 1919, Louis Kaufmann & Sons, Baltimore, Md., $40-50

The B. C. & A. Depot.   OCEAN CITY. Md.

The B. C. & A. Depot, Hand Colored.

#8026—postmarked 1913, for F. J. Harmonson, $50+

R. R. Station, Ocean City, Md.

1909 message to Mrs. Jones,

"We are having a grand time down here. Don't want to go home a bit. Expect to though on Monday as we got a ten day ticket. We have great fun bathing. With love, Hoke"

B. C. & A. R. R. STATION, OCEAN CITY, MD.

#8030—CT production code 1916, Louis Kaufmann & Sons, Baltimore, Md., $40-50

#8030a—c. 1910, H. C. Monroe, McDaniel, Md., $60+

B. C. & A. Wharf, Claiborne, Md.

The steamboat portion of the trip is outlined in blue; the train route in red. The visible lines on this 1916 map represent railroad tracks. No auto roads were shown.

Bathing Beauty—Baltimore, Chesapeake & Atlantic Railway Advertisement—one of a set of early advertising cards put out by the B., C., & A. A ticket could be purchased to leave Baltimore or Annapolis by steamboat for Claiborne, Md. where one connected with the B. C. & A. train to complete the journey to Ocean City.

#8030b—postmarked 1906, The Peters Pub. & Ptg. Co., Balto., $20-25

Handsomely Illustrated Summer Resort Book (96 pages), Descriptive of OCEAN CITY, MARYLAND, and containing list of Hotels and Boarding Houses, sent on receipt of six cents postage. Address, T. Murdoch, Gen'l Passenger Agent. BALTIMORE, CHESAPEAKE & ATLANTIC RAILWAY, Pier 2 Light Street, Baltimore, Md.

The Railroad Entrance to Ocean City.

The Railroad entrance to Ocean City, Md.

#8028 postmarked 1909, Spetzler, Connor, & Coffin, Made in Germany, $30-40

ON THE BOARDWALK, OCEAN CITY, MD.

#8031—c. 1915, Tichnor Bros., Cambridge, Mass., $10-12

JESTER'S SOUVENIR, CONFECTIONERY AND LUNCH PAVILION, OCEAN CITY, MD.

#8033—c. 1915, Tichnor Bros., Cambridge, Mass., $20-25

#8032 – c. 1915, publisher unknown, $15-20

Horn's Salt Water Taffy Stand.

1938 message to Teresa,

"Dear Teresa, Am having a swell time here
at the beach. The surf is plenty high and
the swimming is very good.
Love to all, Jane"

Boardwalk, Ocean City, Md.

U. S. COAST GUARD AND BOARDWALK, OCEAN CITY, MD.

#8036—postmarked 1928, Tichnor Bros., Cambridge, Mass., $15-20

No. 215.
Entrance to Ocean City Pier, Ocean City, Md.

BOARDWALK, OCEAN CITY, MD.

Windsor Resort, D. Trimper, Proprietor.

#8037a—postmarked 1911, Pub. By Spetzler, Connor, & Coffin,
Printed by Baltimore Stationery Co., Baltimore, Md., $15-20

#8035—CT production code 1916, Louis Kaufmann & Sons, Baltimore, Md., $15-20

#8037—c. 1920, Tichnor Bros., Cambridge, Mass., $25-30

BOARD WALK AND PAVILION FROM LIFE SAVING STATION, OCEAN CITY, MD.

1934 message to May,

"Came down last Friday and find the ocean as thrilling as ever. Ann is brown as a berry and I have changed color too. Busy days—will write when I get back to town next week. Love, Violet"

Boardwalk—Maryland Pharmacy.

BOARD WALK, OCEAN CITY, MD.

#8034—postmarked 1921, Louis Kaufmann & Sons, Baltimore, Md., $10-15

OCEAN CITY PIER AND BOARDWALK. OCEAN CITY. MD.

#8038—CT production code 1923, Louis Kaufmann & Sons, Baltimore, Md., $15-20

#8039—postmarked 1919, The Chessler Co., Baltimore, Md., $25-30

The Pier, Ocean City, Md.

1936 message to Millard,

"Am having one glorious vacation here. We have been to beach party and had a swell time. It is terrible to see the hours I am keeping. Oh well, all in a lifetime. Frances"

Moving Pictures, Dancing, Bowling Alleys.

No 218.   Pier at Ocean City, Md.

#8041—c. 1910, Pub. By Spetzler, Connor, & Coffin, Printed by Baltimore Stationery Co., Baltimore, Md., $15-20

#8040—c. 1915, publisher unknown, $15-20

Ocean City Pier, Ocean City, Md.

20704

1947 message to Robert,

"We went out on the pier last night and looked at the shark. One is quite large, the others like large hardheads. But they are catching few fish. Marian"

1945 message to Aunt Irene,

"We are certainly enjoying ourselves here in Ocean City. We get plenty of food and rest. I took Pat O'Connor to a jitterbug palace named Jackson's last night. Love, Harry"

1938 message to Mrs. Pett,

"This place is way larger than Rehoboth although same size dot on the map. Took me one hour to come here. Will shop around pricing rooms. Can't do worse for $1.50. If satisfactory will go back to Rehoboth for my things and come here for tonight and maybe Friday night. They have rolling chairs on the boardwalk here and amuse-ments. Stanley"

1946 message to Cecil,

"Roses are red
Violets are blue
The beach is wonderful
I'm tanned clear through

Having fun???
Yes—Me too.
Georgina"

#8045—c. 1925, publisher unknown, $15-20

#8043—c. 1920, Tichnor Bros., Cambridge, Mass., $15-20

#8044—CT production code 1913, Louis Kaufmann & Sons, Baltimore, Md., $20-25

LOOKING FROM THE PIER, OCEAN CITY, MD.

98

BAND CONCERT, OCEAN CITY, MD.

#8042—c. 1925, publisher unknown, $20-25

Looking South from the Pier.

No. 1102   LOOKING SOUTH FROM THE PIER, OCEAN CITY, MD.   Copyrighted 1906 by Geo. B. Conner

#8047—Copyrighted 1906 by Geo. B. Conner, $10-15

#8046—postmarked 1919, The Chessler Co., Baltimore, Md, $20-25

1949 message to Eileen,

"This is a lovely long beach with big breakers coming in and we are enjoying the sound of water whishing all the time. A mite cool for swimming but we are hoping for warmer weather. Eleanor"

Rolling Chairs, Ocean City, Md.

When the tide comes in at
Ocean City, Md.

595-1

#8048—postmarked 1911, publisher unknown, $8-10

1943 message to Sarah,

"The trip down wasn't too awful. The kids are having a wonderful time and Benny ate a huge dinner after really enjoying his swim. They are certainly a couple of live wires. I wish you were here to help me. Carolyn"

OCEAN CITY, MD.

ON THE BOARDWALK, OCEAN CITY, MD.

1933 message to Sarah,

"We were here last Sunday. The lady on the boardwalk took my picture. With Love, Henry"

#8049—c. 1930, boardwalk photographer, $10-15

#8050—dated 1933, boardwalk photographer, $15-20

Horse & Buggies on Beach with Dog.

THE BEACH AND PIER, OCEAN CITY, MD.

#8048a—Copyright 1907 by Sudwarth Co., Washington, D.C., $15-20

1952 message to Mrs. Mabel,

"The breeze here is something to rave about and the water is actually cold. Am doing some tall relaxing. Mary & B."

#8052—postmarked 1906, Washington Pharmacy, Ocean City, Md., No. 1883 by Franz Huld, New York, $15-20

1952 message to Mr. & Mrs. Wolford,

"Really enjoying ourselves. The waters fine. The sea breeze floats into our room and boy can we sleep; Love, Betty & Milt"

No. 1883 Washington Pharmacy, Ocean City, Md

Sept. 29, 1906.

You remember the Plim?

Yrs. S. Utch.

The Plimhimmon, Ocean City, Md.

1914 message to Mr. Cromwell,

"Hada fine sail on the bay in a catboat on Thursdaywith 8 other Baltimore teachers and my newSharpsburg Friend. Also, one be-foresix on Friday morn-ing with Miss Mary. Have been out in the beach chairs, too. Lovingly, Nellie"

No. 1885. Franz Huld, Publisher, New York

Fishing at Ocean City, Md.

#8053—c. 1906, No. 1885 by Franz Huld, New York, $15-20

Train Crossing the Sinepuxent Bay.

#8054—postmarked 1906, No. 1881 by Franz Huld, New York, $25-30

#8055—c. 1906, No. 1886 by Franz Huld, New York, $10-15

Sailboat on Sinepuxent Bay.

Train Crossing Sinepuxent Bay at Ocean City, Md.

This is the way to get to O. C. Very desolate and artistic right now. D. M. H.

The Sinepuxent Bay at Ocean City, Md.

Bird's Eye View looking North.

Bird's Eye View looking South.

#8058—c. 1910, Spetzler, Connor, & Coffin, Made in Germany, $20-25

#8056—c. 1910, Spetzler, Connor, & Coffin, Made in Germany, $20-25

The Electric Power House and Surrounding.

#8057—postmarked 1910, Spetzler, Connor, & Coffin, Made in Germany, $25-30

Greetings from Ocean City

#8060—c. 1910, Paul Finkenrath, Berlin, $15-20

1936 message to Mr. & Mrs. Crowder,

"If you could see me I am sure you could not believe anyone could get so sunburned in one day as I have to-day. We are having a wonderful time. Believe me I am ready for three meals after going in the water twice a day. Mary Frances"

1938 message to "The Telephone Girls, Star Telephone Co., Wadsworth, Ohio,

"Having a wonderful time. We went sailing this A.M. Have invitation to go deep sea fishing Wed. with a party on a private yacht. Bathing is swell, have to watch waves or you get knocked for a loop. Doris and Mildred"

Greetings from Ocean City, Md.

Bathing at Ocean City, Md.

#8064—postmarked 1910, publisher unknown, $20-25

1938 message to Peggy,

"I'll be home in a few days. I am as brown as a berry. It is swell down here, I wish you were here. I go in bathing every day. Love Diddy"

Beach Scene at Ocean City, Md.

#8065—c. 1910, publisher unknown, $15-20

Sailing on the Synepuxent Bay, Ocean City, Md.

#8067—postmarked 1908, Spetzler, Connor, & Coffin, Made in Germany, $10-12

WRECK OF THE "JOHN W. HALL,"
CAPT. W. H. BENNETT,
STRANDED MAR. 11TH, 1912.
AT OCEAN CITY, MD.

#8066—dated 1912, L. Kaufmann & Sons, Baltimore, Md., $30-40

Boardwalk and Auditorium—Lace & Linen Store.

1929 message to Gilbert,

"Wish you were here now to go in for a swim. Have enjoyed the ocean breezes so much. Am lucky so far—2 weeks and no rain. Came down by Annapolis, but will go home by way of Rehoboth Beach and Wilmington. Best Wishes, J. W."

#8071—CT production code 1931, Louis Kaufmann & Sons, Baltimore, Md., $15-20

#8059—c. 1915, publisher unknown, $10-15

1913 message to Miss Darcy,

"I'm sorry I have to leave here so soon. This is the new school house. Very good looking inside and view of the ocean and bay. With love, Bertha"

OCEAN CITY STATE SCHOOL. OCEAN CITY, MD.

#8072—c. 1935, R. D. Driscoll, Ocean City, Md., The Albertype Co., Brooklyn, N.Y., $10-15

CONVENTION HALL AND PIER   OCEAN CITY, MARYLAND

109

1942 message to Peggy,

"My soldier friend is neat. I stayed on duty with him yesterday for 2 hrs, then we went in bathing. He got changed to beach patrol I think. I am looking for him now. Love, Diddy"

ATLANTIC HOTEL

Copyright, 1906, C. F. Coffin

Atlantic Hotel—Seahorse Border.

#8068—Copyright 1906, C. F. Coffin, Ocean City, Md., $15-20

Coffin's Pharmacy & Bazaar.

#8069—Copyright 1904, C. F. Coffin, Ocean City, Md., $20-25

Atlantic Avenue—Sailboat Multi-View.

#8070—Copyright 1904, C. F. Coffin, Ocean City, Md., $15-20

BALTO. AVE LOOKING NORTH

GREETINGS FROM OCEAN CITY, MD.

SAINT PAUL BY THE SEA

COFFIN'S PHARMACY & BAZAAR

Copyright, 1904, C. F. Coffin

ATLANTIC AVE. LOOKING NORTH

GREETINGS FROM OCEAN CITY, MD.

ATLANTIC AVE. LOOKING NORTH

ATLANTIC AVE. LOOKING NORTH

Copyright, 1904, C. F. Coffin

1.—BOARDWALK AND BEACH AT U. S. COAST GUARD STATION. OCEAN CITY. MD.

#8073—c. 1945, Harry P. Cann & Bros. Co., Baltimore, Md., $10-15

Showell's Bowling Alleys and Fountain.

Boardwalk Looking North   Ocean City, Maryland

#8072a—c. 1935, R. D. Driscoll, Ocean City, Md., The Albertype Co., Brooklyn, N.Y., $10-15

#8072b—c. 1935, R. D. Driscoll, Ocean City, Md., The Albertype Co., Brooklyn, N.Y., $10-15

Boardwalk South from the Valhalla   Ocean City, Maryland

1951 message to Helen,

"This is the kind of life for us. All you do is eat, rest & relax in the sun. The ocean has been wonderful. Rough & Cool. Hope you are well. Pib"

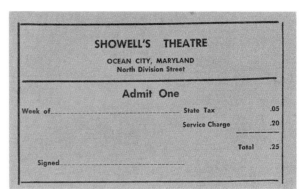

SHOWELL'S   THEATRE

OCEAN CITY, MARYLAND
North Division Street

Admit One

Week of		State Tax	.05
		Service Charge	.20
		Total	.25
Signed			

#8073e—$2-3

1917 message to Mrs. K,

"Had a 228 mile auto trip from Baltimore on wonderful roads."

1952 message to the Bell family,

"Having a grand time—weather and water A+, except the ocean seems to be working off a grudge on everyone who ventures in. The Woodeys"

#8074—CT production code 1914, Louis Kaufmann & Sons, Baltimore, Md., $10-12

#8075—c. 1930, publisher unknown, $8-10

Photographer on Boardwalk.

BOARD WALK AND COTTAGES, OCEAN CITY, MD.

1952 message to the Dygarts,

"Still can't believe we have Lloyd on a vacation, and he's really enjoying it. Ocean is beautiful, but beach is hot! Gladys & Lloyd"

LOOKING NORTH ON BOARDWALK FROM OCEAN CITY PIER, OCEAN CITY, MD.

#8076—postmarked 1922, Louis Kaufmann & Sons, Baltimore, Md., $10-15

1950 message to Sister Hemelt,

"Having a grand time at the sea shore. Children love the water and are contented. Baby loves the boardwalk. Love Ginny"

#8077—postmarked 1925, Louis Kaufmann & Sons, Baltimore, Md., $10-15

#8078—c. 1930, Chessler & Oberender, Baltimore, Md., $10-12

Boardwalk showing Coast Guard Lookout, Ocean City, Md.

BOARDWALK, LOOKING NORTH FROM No. 8 COAST GUARD STATION, OCEAN CITY, MD.

BALTIMORE AVENUE, OCEAN CITY, MD.

Baltimore Avenue—Ice Cream Parlor.

#8079—postmarked 1928, Tichnor Bros., Cambridge, Mass., $15-20

#8080—c. 1930, publisher unknown, $10-15

BALTIMORE AVENUE, SHOWING AUTO LINE, OCEAN CITY, MD.

#8081—CT production code 1916, Louis Kaufmann & Sons, Baltimore, Md., $20-25

Baltimore Ave., Ocean City, Md.

1948 message to Miss Mary,

"I do hope you and Grannie have been comfortable in all the heat. I do wish I could send you some ocean breezes. Love, Hattie"

114

#8083—c. 1920, publisher unknown, $20-25

Ferris Wheel and Swing, Ocean City, Md.

1920s era card with message from one child to another,

"I am having a great time down here. Playing in the sand, riding the flying horses and a thing they call the whip. Robert"

#8084a— c 1925, publisher unknown, $10-12

THE WHIP AND FERRIS WHEEL, OCEAN CITY, MD.

BOARDWALK, BEACH AND COAST GUARD STATION   OCEAN CITY, MARYLAND

#8087—c. 1935, R. D. Driscoll, Ocean City, Md., The Albertype Co., Brooklyn, N.Y., $10-15

SYNEPUXENT BAY BRIDGE   APPROACH TO OCEAN CITY, MARYLAND

#8086—postmarked 1937, R. D. Driscoll, Ocean City, Md., The Albertype Co., Brooklyn, N.Y., $15-20

#8084b— c 1925, publisher unknown, $8-10

A Happy Crowd on the Beach, Ocean City, Md.

1963 message to Mrs. Michelson,

*"Our room isn't the most modern but the food is good & unusual. We had soft crabs last night, bacon & eggs for breakfast & roast lamb for lunch. We're on the beach now.
Love, C. A. & Margie"*

VIEW OF BEACH AND AMUSEMENT SECTION, OCEAN CITY, MD.

#8082—Postmarked 1918, Louis Kaufmann & Sons, Baltimore, Md., $10-15

23:-BOARDWALK AND BEACH AT ATLANTIC HOTEL AND OCEAN PIER, OCEAN CITY, MD.

43913

#8088—c. 1945, Harry P. Cann & Bros. Co., Baltimore, Md., $8-10

1953 message to 'Pimlico' Employees of Union Trust Co. in Baltimore,

"Hi Gang, Am having a swell time as I write this. I am thinking of you Dolls working? Ha. Ha. Do all the work before I return OK? Will see you all next week. Caroline"

#8085—CT production code 1916, Louis Kaufmann & Sons, Baltimore, Md., $20-25

THE CASINO THEATRE, OCEAN CITY, MD.

THE HAMILTON   OCEAN CITY, MARYLAND

#8088c—postmarked 1938, R. D. Driscoll, Ocean City, Md., The Albertype Co., Brooklyn, N.Y., $10-15

Bathing Beach of Atlantic Hotel

Bathing Beach of Atlantic Hotel
—Hand Colored.

#8090—c. 1935, The Albertype Co., Brooklyn, N.Y., $10-15

Hamilton Hotel—Hand Colored.

#8088b—c. 1935, Hand Colored, The Albertype Co., Brooklyn, N.Y., $10-15

#8088a—c. 1925, publisher unknown, $10-12

Hamilton Hotel, Ocean City, Md.

HAMILTON HOTEL
Directly on the Boardwalk at 3rd Street
Ocean City, Maryland

ATLANTIC HOTEL, OCEAN CITY, MD.

#8089—CT production code 1914, Louis Kaufmann & Sons, Baltimore, Md., $10-15

ATLANTIC HOTEL   OCEAN CITY, MARYLAND

#8091—c. 1935, The Albertype Co., Brooklyn, N.Y., $15-20

#8092—c. 1935, R. D. Driscoll, Ocean City, Md., The Albertype Co., Brooklyn, N.Y., $10-15

1956 message to Miss Helen,

"We will drive to Rehoboth today to look it over and get back in time for a swim and the beach. It is 28 miles each way. Having a fine time. Julia"

1934 message to Lena,

"My wish is to bring you down here for at least four days to sit right in this ole ocean and salt yourself down. Love Elmer & Hilda"

ATLANTIC HOTEL   OCEAN CITY, MARYLAND

Colonial Hotel—1909.

Colonial Hotel, Ocean City, Md.

#8093—postmarked 1909, Rinn Publ. Co., Balto., Md., $15-20

Colonial Hotel—1924.

COLONIAL HOTEL, OCEAN CITY, MD.

#8095—postmarked 1924, Tichnor Bros., Cambridge, Mass., $8-10

#8094—postmarked 1918, Louis Kaufmann & Sons, Baltimore, Md., $10-15

Colonial Hotel—1918.

The Colonial Hotel, Ocean City, Md.

COLONIAL

Colonial Hotel—1940—Real Photo.

#8096—c. 1940, processed by DOPS, $30-35

COLONIAL

The New Avelon, Ocean City, Md.

#8099—postmarked 1911, Pub. By Spetzler, Coffin, & Connor, Printed by Baltimore Stationery Co., Baltimore, Md., $10-15

1914 message to William,

"The boardwalk is 24 feet wide and more than a mile long. When too tired to walk one can hire a chair on wheels and be pushed along by a negro at 50 cts. an hour. Bathing is good along the beach. I have been attending the annual meeting of the State Teachers Association. Fare 3.50 round trip from Baltimore. Got 1.00 a day rate New Avelon Hotel. Yours truly, S. E. Grose"

Hotel Stephen Decatur—Hand Colored.

#8097—postmarked 1933, The Albertype Co., Brooklyn, N.Y., $10-15

1922 message to Mary,

"We are down here having a fine time. We drove down in a Franklin sedan with friends. We all went in the ocean bathing before breakfast. Edna"

The Mount Pleasant Hotel,
Ocean City, Md.

#8101—c. 1925, Tichnor Bros., Cambridge, Mass., $10-12

#8098—postmarked 1914, Louis Kaufmann & Sons, Baltimore, Md., $10-15

The Belmont Hotel and Cottages,
Ocean City, Md.

#8100—postmarked 1914, Louis Kaufmann & Sons, Baltimore, Md., $10-15

The Lankford Hotel, Ocean City, Md.

1925 message to Mrs. Tucker,

"I am having a glorious time bathing, sailing, crabbing, dancing, going to movies, laughing, reading, sleeping, eating, talking with friends, walking, etc. Love to all, Agnes"

#8103—postmarked 1926, publisher unknown, $8-10

#8102—c. 1925, Tichnor Bros., Cambridge, Mass., $15-20

AVONDALE HOTEL, OCEAN CITY, MD.

1938 message to Miss Anna,

"Tell your Mother she & you should be here. The salt water is really good for corns. Will see you. Dycie"

The Idylwild, Ocean City, Md.

#8104—c. 1925, The Chessler Co., Baltimore, Md., $10-15

1938 message to Mrs. Goettling,

"Had a lovely trip down to the ocean. The ocean looks great. There are 64 people registered at the Hastings Hotel. Love, Hattie"

#8106—CT production code 1928, Louis Kaufmann & Sons, Baltimore, Md., $10-15

#8107—c. 1925, Tichnor Bros., Cambridge, Mass., $15-20

SEASIDE HOTEL, OCEAN CITY, MD.

NEW MT. PLEASANT HOTEL, OCEAN CITY

HASTINGS HOTEL, OCEAN CITY, MD.

#8108—CT production code 1923, Louis Kaufmann & Sons, Baltimore, Md., $10-15

MARYLAND INN, OCEAN CITY, MD.

#8109—CT production code 1923, Louis Kaufmann & Sons, Baltimore, Md., $10-15

#8110—postmarked 1929, Louis Kaufmann & Sons, Baltimore, Md., $10-15

1961 message to Mrs. McCleary,

"We arrived safe & sound about eight o'clock, the ride was cool. Had breakfast at the "Hastings". Apt. is O.K., Irma"

COTTAGES AND KAY HOTEL, OCEAN CITY, MD.

122955

The Mt. Pleasant & Virginia Hotels, Ocean City, Md.

1967 message to Mr. & Mrs. Crawford,

"Greetings—Surprised how much I am really enjoying this apartment. Just rocking on porch watching ocean and bathers. Hope your trip to the farm did you a lot of good. Raymond – Marie"

#8111—c. 1925, The Chessler Co., Baltimore, Md., $10-15

#8112—postmarked 1923, Louis Kaufmann & Sons, Baltimore, Md., $10-15

1961 message to Mrs. Wagoner,
(back of Plimhimmon Hotel card),

"I am having a real nice time. This is a beautiful hotel. Meals are fine. They serve two meals a day. I came here on account of elevator service. Wish your mother was here with me. Nettie"

HOTEL PLINHIMMON, OCEAN CITY, MD.

1939 message to Grace,

"Ruth is raring to go. Can't wait till dinner is over. I'm not going in till Thursday. Have to get my nerve up. Doubt if I get any more than my toes wet. Margaret"

DEL MAR VA HOTEL   BALTIMORE AVENUE   OCEAN CITY, MARYLAND

#8113-CT production code 1923, Louis Kaufmann & Sons, Baltimore, Md., $8-10

#8114—c. 1935, R. D. Driscoll, Ocean City, Md., The Albertype Co., Brooklyn, N.Y., $10-15

SHOREHAM HOTEL, OCEAN CITY, MD.

1942 message to Mrs. Bryan,

"This is the life—you really would appreciate it. Why don't you jump in the car & come down. Gladys"

1955 message to
Reverend & Mrs. Manley,

*"This is where we attended Church
& S.S. on Sunday. Had a very nice
service. Will & Lottie"*

#8115—CT production code 1923, Louis Kaufmann & Sons, Baltimore, Md., $10-15

#8116—c. 1925, Tichnor Bros., Cambridge, Mass., $10-15

DR. TOWNSEND COTTAGE, OCEAN CITY, MD.

1963 message to Sister Agnes,

*"Vacation time again—Rode
down to Our Lady of the Sea
Church on a bicycle & said the
Stations. Josephine"*

1910 message to Jennie,

"This is the church in which I have a nice class of girls to teach for the summer. I am writing this at half past six on the evening Roy left here. He will tell you that I want three more skeins of the green silk. Love to all. Cousin Emily"

ST. MARY'S STAR OF THE SEA, OCEAN CITY, MD.

#8117—postmarked 1911, Pub. By Spetzler, Coffin, & Connor, Printed by Baltimore Stationery Co., Baltimore, Md., $10-15

#8118—CT production code 1923, Louis Kaufmann & Sons, Baltimore, Md., $8-10

St. Paul's Episcopal Church, Ocean City, Md.

1955 message to Chas.,

"Dear Charlie, We are beginning to plan to close up here. I finished one coat of white paint on porch & Z fence panels out front. I have been S.S. Supt. at the little church for 2 Sundays & teach the lesson every Sunday. Love to all, Rue"

Rapid Transit, near Ocean City, Md.

#8119—postmarked 1918, Louis Kaufmann & Sons, Baltimore, Md., $10-15

1948 message to Miss Ida,

"We are down here on vacation. It is very quiet here compared to Atlantic City or Wildwood. Catherine and Bill and Billy"

#8120—Copyright 1908, by A. Q. Southwick, N.Y., $6-8

1935 message to Wes and Grace,

"We have had a lovely week here and a grand time. Gene has done a lot of fishing and has caught quite a few. We leave tomorrow, much to my regret. Love, Helen"

When I say the change is quite too lovely for words, This embraces everything

N.15-B   Design Copyright, 1908, by A. Q. Southwick, N.Y.

Fishing Party with the Dunns—Real Photo.

1957 message to Mr. & Mrs. Lucas,

"Last night someone landed a blue marlin about 5 feet long. In the evening there are millions of charter fishing and cruising boats in the harbor. We went up to the boardwalk last night. Love Ronnie, Laurie, Gary

BEGINS MAY 16th
DEEP SEA FISHING $4.00
$5.00 SAT., SUN., HOLIDAYS

ENDS SEPTEMBER 13th
Cut Bait and Lines Free
ONE TRIP DAILY

Ocean City Yacht Basin, Ocean City, Md.

Capt. Ed. Brex - Phone 583 & 576

PISCES

LEAVES 8 a. m. Returns 3 p. m. or later. Accomodations for Ladies

"CRUISER BOB-JOE"
Capt. Raymond Savage
Ocean City, Md. — Phone 317

11319

131

A Youthful Fisherman Ocean City, Md.

6888

#8124—postmarked 1939, Dexter Press, Pearl River, N.Y., $10-15

#8125—c. 1940, Newton Manufacturing Company, Newton, Iowa, $20-25

#8125a—postmarked 1956, Walter Gray, Hollywood, Florida, $8-10

MAGEE YACHT BASIN, PHONE 576, OCEAN CITY, MARYLAND

O-444

Cruiser Welcome—Captain Russ Kline—For sport fishing all tackle is aboard—Phone 324—Ocean City.

#8126—postmarked 1944, R. D. Driscoll, Ocean City, Md., The Albertype Co., Brooklyn, N.Y., $10-15

1944 message to Mrs. Spickwall,

"Harrison is feeling good. He caught 5 black bass off shore on the bay this morning. I think he is going to be spending most of his time fishing. We went fishing off this wharf, but no luck. Love, Stella"

Headboat Answer—Enjoy our Porgy and Bass fishing, also spinning for Weak fish when practicable. Bring your lunch. Soft drinks and beer aboard. No whiskey or beer may be brought aboard. Capt. Paul Russell—Phone 738-M.

#8126a—c. 1950, E. B. Thomas, Cambridge, Mass., $8-10

#8126b—CT production code 1951, Harry P. Cann & Bros. Co., Baltimore, Md., $6-8

Fishing from the Pier.

"ANSWER" AT OCEAN CITY. MD. - NOTED FOR BEST FISHING

Boats in the Harbor, Ocean City, Maryland

17

#8127—postmarked 1946, Tichnor Bros., Cambridge, Mass., $3-4

1940 message to Elenna,

"We are tied up at the dock here and having a grand storm. Just finished walking the boardwalk and had our dinner. Back on the boat just before the rain. Love, Adele & Harold"

#8128—CT production code 1939, Harry P. Cann & Bros. Co., Baltimore, Md., $6-8

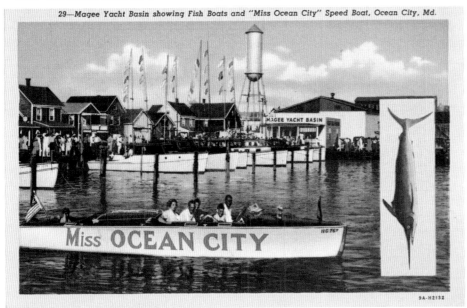

29—Magee Yacht Basin showing Fish Boats and "Miss Ocean City" Speed Boat, Ocean City, Md.

9A-H2152

#8129—CT production code 1953, Harry P. Cann & Bros. Co., Baltimore, Md., $4-5

29—Ocean City Yacht Basin, showing Fishing Boats, Ocean City, Md.

3C-H1300

6—U. S. Coast Guard Lookout Tower at Inlet, Ocean City, Md.

#8130—CT production code 1940, Harry P. Cann & Bros. Co., Baltimore, Md., $4-5

OB-H2202

1952 message to Mrs. Huffer,

"It's hot here too, but there is a good air and sleeping is pleasant. You should be here. Mary"

1950 message to George,

"No job, bad sunburn, no food, no money, but one heck of a good time. No kidding, its great. The beach is full of sand fleas and there's a girl for every flea. Bob"

#8131—c. 1945, Tichnor Bros., Cambridge, Mass., $6-8

GREETINGS from OCEAN CITY

#8132—c. 1945, Edwards Stores Inc., $6-8

#8133—CT production code 1939, Harry P. Cann & Bros. Co., Baltimore, Md., $6-8

#8134—CT production code 1944, Harry P. Cann & Bros. Co., Baltimore, Md., $8-10

1963 message to Mrs. Butts,

"Having a nice time. Went to the beach today, going tomorrow so Cody can look at the girls. Love, Bettie"

24—Boardwalk and Beach, Looking North from Coast Guard Station, Ocean City, Md.

1B-H2180

1951 message to Mr. & Mrs. Garman,

"We are having a perfectly grand vacation this year. Each day seems better than the previous one. Love, Pat & Flora"

#8136—CT production code 1941, Harry P. Cann & Bros. Co., Baltimore, Md., $6-8

#8137—CT production code 1939, Harry P. Cann & Bros. Co., Baltimore, Md., $6-8

#8135—CT production code 1941, Harry P. Cann & Bros. Co., Baltimore, Md., $8-10

10—Amusement Center and Boardwalk, Ocean City, Md.

1B-H2181

30—Boardwalk and Beach North from Roosevelt Hotel, Ocean City, Md.

9A-H2133

We're Warming up Waiting for you
Ocean City, Maryland

#8138—postmarked 1941, Tichnor Bros., Cambridge, Mass., $8-10

1940 message to Mrs. Lofland
(in the large print of a child),

"We visited this place Sunday and other places. Fenwick Island, Bethany Beach, Dewey Beach and Rehoboth. Had a fine time. First trip we have had this summer. Edna"

#8139—c. 1945, Edwards Stores Inc., $8-10

1947 message to Mr. and Mrs. Arthur,

"Hello Folks. Arrived O.K—1 P.M. ate dinner out—then went on the beach. M & G like the water. Bob does not. He loves the sand. We are on the beach now. I am writing this on a beach ball—some table.
Love to all, Dot"

On the Boardwalk, at Ocean City, Md.

5:–UNITED STATES COAST GUARD STATION, OCEAN CITY, MD.

43895

#8140—c. 1940, Harry P. Cann & Bros. Co., Baltimore, Md., $8-10

1956 message to Mrs. Arnold,

"Spending a long weekend at the Royalton with our friends from Fairfax, Va. Have been biking on the boardwalk and swimming, but the ocean is quite cold. Love, Glad & Bill"

U. S. Coast Guard Station showing "duck" boat.

1945 message to Mary N,

"I am at the shore and I am having a swell time. There are seven girls down here and what a time. Love Mary B"

5—U. S. Coast Guard Station, Ocean City, Md.

#8141—CT production code 1953, Photo by Walter Gray of Hollywood, Harry P. Cann & Bros. Co., Baltimore, Md., $10-15

28—Dominican College, Ocean City, Md.

9A-H2131

#8142—CT production code 1939, Harry P. Cann & Bros. Co., Baltimore, Md., $6-8

1939 message to Mrs. Parrish,

"Hope you have had enough rain so that you haven't had to water our garden. It is raining here now. We are staying at a quiet hotel (The Del-Mar) and are enjoying it very much. The ocean is almost at our door."

#8143—c. 1950, Eastern Shore News Co., by Beals, Des Moines, Iowa, $6-8

56 OCEAN CITY HIGH SCHOOL, OCEAN CITY, MD.

OCEAN CITY HIGH SCHOOL

1953 message to Lottie, Emma, and Gertrude,

"This is surely a nice place to spend a vacation. We are all ready to go into the ocean. The beauty contest and parade is being held this afternoon. We can't wait to see that. Glenn & Helen"

Dinner-time for the Sea Gulls.   Ocean City, Md

#8141a—postmarked 1947, Tichnor Bros., Boston, Mass., $2-3

1953 message,

"Dear Grandpa, I know you will like the ride over the bay bridge. I will be looking for you Saturday.   Have a nice trip. Love, Ken"

#8144—CT production code 1946, Chesapeake Airways Photo, Harry P. Cann & Bros. Co., Baltimore, Md., $20-25

OC-36—Chesapeake Airways Service Crossing the Chesapeake Bay

From Baltimore to Easton, Salisbury and Ocean City, Md.   CHESAPEAKE AIRWAYS PHOTO

Chesapeake Airways—Service to Ocean City.

1955 message to Mrs. Singer,

"I am having a lazy time staying in the house. I got burnt the second day I was here. Mrs. Peregoy

CHESAPEAKE BAY BRIDGE LINKING EASTERN SHORE WITH ANNAPOLIS, MD.

Chesapeake Bay Bridge—opened to traffic in 1952.

#8145a—c. 1952, The Mayrose Co., Linden, N.J., $4-6

1944 message to Mr. Hammer,

"We did exactly what you said we would do. We were going over on the ferry but missed it. Am having a grand time. Wish you could be along for I know you would be the life of the party. There are plenty of good looking women here.
Love Elizabeth"

Claiborne—Annapolis—Matapeake Ferry.

#8145b—dated 1938, Kodak real photo, Steamship Historical Society of America, Inc., $8-10

CLAIBORNE — ANNAPOLIS — MATAPEAKE FERRY

GOV. HARRY W. NICE

1945 message to Tom,

"Had a very comfortable trip and was cool all the way! The ferry ride of 30 minutes was very pleasant. I got a cup of coffee and sandwich on the boat. Took a taxi to the house. I feel sure we are going to have a good time together. Much love, Mother"

#8146—c. 1955, Clear-Vue, Willens & Co., Chicago, $10-15

1947 message to Catherine,

"We are enjoying the air and the food. Imagine ham and eggs and strawberries and hot cakes all at once if you can. Only irony is did we bring something large enough to wear back. Lydia and Sid"

Knotty Pine Restaurant—*"A full course meal or a sandwich. It's a pleasure to serve you. Doris and Lester Wise."*

#8147—c. 1950, Tingle Printing Co., Pittsville, Md., $6-8

1954 message to Barbara,

"Hello there. We sat along the water last night and watched the moon. Nice and hot here and we are enjoying every minute of it. Verna & Ralph"

1952 message to Edward,

"Its pretty nice down here at Harrison Hall and the ocean is grand. Cool of night. Plenty hot days. The new bridge is a beauty and a wonder. Love to all, Aunt Estelle"

27—Ship Cafe, Ocean City, Md.

9A H2130

#8148—CT production code 1939, Harry P. Cann & Bros. Co., Baltimore, Md., $6-8

1956 message,

"Dear Agnes, The Ship Café in picture is where we always eat dinner on the nite of Emma & John's anniversary. Good eating there. Margaret"

The Ship Café & Pedal Boats.

#8149—c. 1945, Edwards Stores, Inc., $8-10

#8145—CT production code 1944, Harry P. Cann & Bros. Co., Baltimore, Md., $6-8

3—Bridge Spanning the Sinepuxent Bay, Ocean City, Md.

4B-H1129

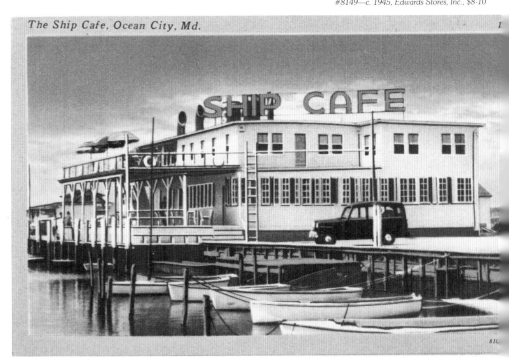

The Ship Cafe, Ocean City, Md.

7—Commander Hotel and Beach, Ocean City, Md.

OB-H2203

#8150—CT production code 1940, Harry P. Cann & Bros. Co., Baltimore, Md., $6-8

Commander Hotel—1940.

1958 message to Marian.

"We're having lots of fun and the water is really great. You should see me ride the big waves on a surf mat. Sue"

#8151—CT production code 1950, Harry P. Cann & Bros. Co., Baltimore, Md., $6-8

7—Commander Hotel, Boardwalk at 14th St., Ocean City, Md.

OC-H105

Commander Hotel—1950.

1943 message to Mrs. Todd,

"We have our room & bath now, in fact, only the first night without bath. We are getting ready now to go out on the beach and loll around for the morning. I may take a dip if I can get a bathing cap of some kind. Best Regards, Ernestine"

8—Maryland Inn, Ocean City, Md.

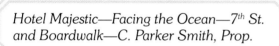

1963 message to Mr. & Mrs. Gordon,

"Tired but happy. Imperial Crab for supper, and no dishes to wash. Tad & Al"

Hotel Majestic—Facing the Ocean—7th St. and Boardwalk—C. Parker Smith, Prop.

HOTEL MAJESTIC   OCEAN CITY, MARYLAND

FACING THE OCEAN   6A-H747

19—Hotel Normandy, Ocean City, Md.

HOTEL DEL-MAR-VA, BALTIMORE AVE., OCEAN CITY, MARYLAND

#8154—c. 1945, Del-Mar-Va Sales Co., Salisbury, Maryland, $8-10

19—Lambros Apartments, Ocean City, Md.

#8156—CT production code 1955, Harry P. Cann & Bros. Co., Baltimore, Md., $10-12

Breakers Hotel—Boardwalk and 3rd St.—
"Eat Well—Sleep Well—And be served well."

#8155—c. 1945, MWM Color-Litho, MWM, Aurora, Mo., $6-8

BREAKERS HOTEL, OCEAN CITY, MARYLAND

1956 message to Mr. & Mrs. Ogden,

"This is where we are and enjoying fine. We are right on the board walk. Shore, amusements, and restaurants. We don't have to use the car just walk out the hotel on to the beach. Love, Sis"

1939 message to Mother,

"We drove thru terrible rain storms on the way down but arrived safely. Today has been glorious—clear and bright. The apartment is darling and we are enjoying it so much. Just finished dinner and are walking to see the sights.
Lovingly, Janet"

11—Neikirk's Apartments, Ocean City, Md.

6B-H1846

The Warren Cottage—409 Boardwalk, Cor. 5th St., Phone 161, Mrs. Robert I. Warren, Owner.

#8157—CT production code 1946, Harry P. Cann & Bros. Co., Baltimore, Md., $10-12

#8158—postmarked 1945, MWM Color-Litho, MWM, Aurora, Mo., $8-10

THE WARREN COTTAGE
Ocean Front
Ocean City, Md.

1945 message to Mrs. Hill
(obviously from a child),

"Dear Aunt Grace, We are here for a couple days. I have really been walking and playing in the sand today. Tomorrow mother is going to get me a bucket & shovel and I expect to dig a big hole.
Love and a kiss, Jeanette"

#8160—postmarked 1958, Edwards Stores, Inc., $8-10

#8159—postmarked 1956, Edwards Stores, Inc., $6-8

38—Monticello Hotel and Dinner Bell Restaurant, Baltimore Avenue at Third Street, Ocean City, Maryland

#8161—CT production code 1947, Harry P. Cann & Bros. Co., Baltimore, Md., $8-10

The Holiday House, Ocean City, Md. 16

1949 message to Mrs. Perkins,

"We are having a swell time. The water is wonderful. Expect you Thurs. We are on Phila. Ave just past the Brass Rail Night Club on right hand side. Love, Nan"

1953 message to Barbs,

"Very similar to Hampton but with a nicer beach and a very nice boardwalk. Love, Mary"

#8161a—c. 1950, Douglas R. Smith, Washington 5, D.C., $6-8

#8162—CT production code 1941, Harry P. Cann & Bros. Co., Baltimore, Md., $6-8

#8163—c. 1945, Del-Mar-Va Sales Co., Salisbury, Maryland, $8-10

OCEAN CITY, MARYLAND

#8164—c. 1945, processed by EKC, $25-30

Aerial Real Photo.

1936 message to Mrs. Morgan,
(accompanying a similar aerial view)

"Finally accomplished it! Ocean is to the right—and island is two miles long"

1950 message to Mrs. Buchter,

"Hello Mother, Had rain all day so we aren't doing very much but listening to the radio. Pat misses television. Just took Pat and Denny to the movies. Love—Helen & Roy"

Aerial Real Photo—Inlet.

#8165—postmarked 1947, Camera-Gift Shop, $30-40

OCEAN CITY, MARYLAND   CAMERA-GIFT SHOP

KEYSTONE COTTAGES - WEST OCEAN CITY - PHONE 421

#8166—c. 1955, Tingle Printing Company, Pittsville, Md., $8-10

Keystone Cottages—1 mile from Ocean City—Route 707—Phone 421—Mrs. Kathryn Lamar, Owner.

1959 message to Jimmie,

"You don't know what the beach is until you come here. These waves are higher than we are. The beach is even longer than you can see. You better talk Mom into taking you some place like this. See you soon.
Johnnie & Suzie"

Kelly's Market and Cottages—Route 2—Berlin, Md.—Phone Ocean City 0459W2.

KELLY'S COTTAGES—U.S. 50—2 MI. WEST OF OCEAN CITY

#8168—c. 1955, American Skyviews, Chicago, $10-15

#8169—c. 1950, for Brotherhood of St. Andrew, Ocean City, Md., by The Albertype Co., Brooklyn, N.Y., $10-12

Edgewater Apartments   North Ocean City, Maryland

MARYLAND MOTEL & COTTAGES · R.D. No. 1 · Box 425 · Ocean City, Md.

#8167—c. 1965, National Press, Inc., Chicago, $8-10

1951 message to Mrs. Thomas,

"I practice in the morning, swim in the afternoon, & go out at night. Gail"

Maridel Beach Motel & Cottages—Phone 665-J—A. Percy Holland and Elvine S. Holland, Owners and Operators.

#8170—postmarked 1958, Photo and artwork by Douglas R. Smith, Washington, D.C., $8-10

MARIDEL BEACH ... Highway 528 ... NORTH OCEAN CITY, MARYLAND

1961 message to Mrs. Ball,

"It poured all day yesterday & I went out and walked the beach at 7 before many were up. It is really lovely after a storm. Hope for good weather for us. Pinkie"

Ocean City as You Remember It

#8172—postmarked 1954, Photo and artwork by Douglas R. Smith, Washington, D.C., $8-10

North Winds Motel and Apartments   All 30 Units Have Cross Ventilation—V. R. Strickland and E. C. Townsend, Owners and Operators

Elk Horn Tourist Cottages—Hot & Cold Running Water—Cool, Shady, Restful—Playground for Children—Mr. & Mrs. John L. Donaway, Owners and Managers.

#8173—c. 1950, Tingle Printing Co., Pittsville, Marryland, $6-8

Villa-Nova Tourist Cottages—Hot and Cold Water—Private Showers— Innerspring Mattresses—Exclusive Restaurant and Dancing.

#8171—postmarked 1941, Colourpicture, Cambridge, Mass., $10-12

The Miami Court—Philadelphia Ave. at 22nd St.

THE MIAMI COURT, largest motel in Ocean City, Md.

#8175—c. 1950, Yorkolor Process, New York 12, N. Y., $8-10

#8176—c. 1960, Tingle Printing Co., Pittsville, Md., $6-8

Ocean Park Motel—On the Boardwalk at 17th St.
—Telephone Ocean City 1060.

#8176a—c. 1960, Photo by F. W. Brueckmann, Tingle Printing Co., Pittsville, Md., $6-8

1960 message to Mr. Gorrell,

"Having a nice time. I wish you were here. Never a dull moment. Grandma"

Ocean Drive Motel—North Ocean City—
Beach Highway & 69th Street—Tel. Atlantic 9-7630
Owners and Operators: Mr. & Mrs. Gustav Strohsacker.

#8177—postmarked 1961, Tingle Printing Co., Pittsville, Md., $8-10

1957 message to Howard,

"The weather here is fine, just right for vacation. Big day yesterday— fishing in early morning, no fish, golf at Salisbury 10 AM – 2 PM—bad score 106. Then a boat ride on the ocean at 7:30—boardwalk in eve., pinochle till 12—some day—so long. J. G."

#8178—c. 1960, Mardelva News Co., Salisbury, Md., $4-5

Boardwalk looking North.

1959 message to Patricia,

"I am having a real nice time down here at the shore. I got at least a million mosquito bites. I have a pretty nice tan. Love, Barb"

#8174—postmarked 1951, The Albertype Co., Brooklyn, N.Y., $6-8

Miami Motel and Miami Court—Hand Colored—72 Rooms with Tile Showers—Phone 7300.

1971 message to Helen G,

"You watch the waves from one side of the Atlantic and I watch them from the other side. Helen B"

#8179—c. 1965, Color photo by F. W. Brueckmann, Tingle Printing Co., Pittsville, Md., $6-8

1962 message to Mr. Clements,

"We are having a lot of fun. This morning John and I are gone to ride bicycles. Bobby"

Ocean City Beach Patrol Headquarters at Caroline Street.

#8183—postmarked 1967, Color photo by F. W. Brueckmann, Tingle Printing Co., Pittsville, Md., $5-6

#8182—c. 1965, Color photo by F. W. Brueckmann, Tingle Printing Co., Pittsville, Md., $5-6

1958 message to Marilyn and Audrey,

"Having a swell time. Beach is fairly crowded! Feel like a 'hick' walkiing around in bare feet, a custom here! See you soon. Dot"

Sunday Afternoon.

#8185—postmarked 1962, Color photo by F. W. Brueckmann, Tingle Printing Co., Pittsville, Md., $6-8

Lambros Apartments —Boardwalk at 4th St.

"What beautiful music they make to the rhythm and beat of the surf at Ocean City, Maryland."

1954 message to Daddy and Ted,

"Here we are at Ocean City. We have been enjoying the ocean breezes along various stops on the ocean since 11 o'clock this morning."

#8184—c. 1967, Color photo by F. W. Brueckmann, Tingle Printing Co., Pittsville, Md., $8-10

#8186—c. 1965, Photo by Don Ceppi, Mardelva News Co., Salisbury, Md., $6-8

#8187—c. 1965, Color photo by F. W. Brueckmann, Tingle Printing Co., Pittsville, Md., $5-6

#8188—postmarked 1968, Mardelva News Co., Salisbury, Md., $6-8

#8192—c. 1958, Color photo by C. H. Ruth, Tingle Printing Co., Pittsville, Md., $8-10

#8190—c. 1967, Color photo by F. W. Brueckmann, Tingle Printing Co., Pittsville, Md., $5-6

1955 message to Annie,

"Hi Mom, Michael is having a fine
time playing in the sand and water.
Now he is next door playing with
a little boy. The weather is fine.
Always a nice breeze, can sleep
good every night. Lorrisa, Edward &
Michael"

1966 message to Mr./Mrs. Wells,

"Ocean City is grand. We have a nice camp spot under the trees. Cool at night. Lots of air. Went to the beach both days. Lots of fun in the water on the rafts. Went crabbing, but mostly small ones. Jake & Betty"

#8193—c. 1965, Mardelva News Co., Salisbury, Md., $8-10

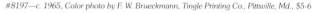

#8197—c. 1965, Color photo by F. W. Brueckmann, Tingle Printing Co., Pittsville, Md., $5-6

Satellite Motel-Boardwalk at 24th St.—
Mr. and Mrs. Ellis Engle and Son, Owners/Managers.

1963 message to Dora,

"We got here about 12 and found a room right away. The sign said 2.00 but we are paying 3.00. The bed is about the only good thing about it. It's clean but it doesn't even have a dresser in it!! Oh, the rugs are right pretty too! We might bring one home! The bus and room together cost $20.33. We are eating up the rest. Barbara"

Amusement Pier showing Loop-O-Plane, Paratrooper, and Octopus.

#8195—c. 1965, Color photos by W. A. Dryden, Eastern Shore Times, $10-15

#8194—c. 1965, Color photo by F. W. Brueckmann, Tingle Printing Co., Pittsville, Md., $5-6

English Diner—22nd St. & Phila. Ave. "As Famous as the Boardwalk."

1962 message to Sister Charlotte at St. Agnes Hospital,

"Sunburnt already! Not as crowded down here as past years. Beach is about half its depth (or width) from that storm. Skip"

Nautilus Apartments—55th St. on the ocean side—
Operated by Mr. & Mrs. Maxwell Quillen.

1950 message to Joanne,

"I drove down here with five others yesterday. Little Diane, 8 years old, had never been to ocean before. Will return home tomorrow, Love Grandma"

#8201—c. 1958, Chuck West, Seaford, Del., $6-8

Ocean Park Motel—Boardwalk at 17th St.

#8196—c. 1958, Chuck West, Washington 16, D.C., $6-8

1962 message to Mrs. Klein,

"Chuck seeing to it that everyone is well rested. Every time we turn around it's nap time. Chuck & children enjoying this terrific pool here. I'm grateful for the splashes that came my way. Chuck, De & Ro, Pat & Andrew"

North Winds Motel

OCEAN CITY, MARYLAND

#8198—c. 1965, Color photo by F. W. Brueckmann, Tingle Printing Co., Pittsville, Md., $5-6

North Winds Motel Pool.

#8199—c. 1962, Color photo by F. W. Brueckmann, Tingle Printing Co., Pittsville, Md., $5-6

#8202—c. 1957, Photo by F. W. Brueckmann and Photolite, Tingle Printing Co., Pittsville, Md., $5-6

Harrington Apartments—Baltimore Ave. & 19th St.— Tel. Atlantic 9-7050.

A 277 lb. blue marlin caught 1957 on The Bolo, Jr. The blue marlin is larger and more rare than the famous fighting white marlin. Ocean City is the world's greatest white marlin fishing center.

#8200—c. 1960, Color photo by F. W. Brueckmann, Tingle Printing Co., Pittsville, Md., $6-8

Greetings from **OCEAN CITY, MARYLAND**

Home of the
WHITE MARLIN

#8204—postmarked 1964, Photo courtesy Capt. Talbot Bunting, Tingle Printing Co., Pittsville, Md., $5-6

1959 message to Lt. Col. Short,

"The rain, wind, fog and cloudiness seems to follow me around—but it's still fun to relax & do nothing at the beach! Love, Gay"

1962 message to Mr. Mann,

"Having a lovely trip, such a large place, tell Mr. Mann he should see the fishing boats bring in these big marlin fish. We saw one 8 feet long. Beautiful place. Mrs. Walker & Charles"

Ocean City, Maryland

#8203—c. 1960, Tichnor Bros., Boston 15, Mass., $4-5

167

#8205—c. 1960, Color photo by F. W. Brueckmann, Tingle Printing Co., Pittsville, Md., $5-6

Aerial View—1950s.

1940 message
in child's handwriting,

"Dear Daddy, We are enjoying
everything. Marie & Bud"

#8211a—c. 1955, Color photo by C. H. Ruth, Tingle Printing Co., Pittsville, Md., $5-6

168

Inside Playland.

Ocean Playland—Playland had a Mad Mouse Ride. It rattled and clanked and shook and shimmied so much, you KNEW the next sharp curve would send you flying off the tracks and into Sinepuxent Bay. Ocean City as I remember it.

#8206—c. 1965, Color photo by F. W. Brueckmann, Tingle Printing Co., Pittsville, Md., $10-12

1957 message to Thelma,

"Sure have had a wonderful time so far, and plenty of fish to eat too. (40 fish, 13 flounders, 1 eel) So you see we had plenty. Pauline"

#8207—c. 1965, Photo by Don Ceppi, Mardelva Distributors, Inc., Salisbury, Md., $15-20

169

Jolly Roger Amusement Park at Night.

Trimper's Amusements—1902 Herschel-Spellman Carousel.

#8209—c. 1965, Photo by Don Ceppi, Mardelva Distributors, Inc., Salisbury, Md., $8-10

Inside Jolly Roger Park.

#8208—c. 1958, Color photo by F. W. Brueckmann, Tingle Printing Co., Pittsville, Md., $4-6

#8210—c. 1965, Photo by Don Ceppi, Mardelva Distributors, Inc., Salisbury, Md., $10-12

1909 message to Miss Handry,

"The campers are here today. We made the trip in the motor boat. The boys are on a search for provisions. Wish you were with us. E. D. P."

#8211—c. 1965, Color photo by F. W. Brueckmann, Tingle Printing Co., Pittsville, Md., $8-10

#8212—postmarked 1966, Color photo by F. W. Brueckmann, Tingle Printing Co., Pittsville, Md., $5-6

1966 message to George,

"I'm suffering from a hang-over and sun-poisoning. Having a great time. Sharon"

Aerial View—1966.

THE OCEAN AND ME

Greetings from Ocean City, Md.

#8213—postmarked 1938, publisher unknown, $5-6

Love's Pilot.

Love's Pilot.

#8214 – c.1910, Raphael Tuck & Sons, Printed in Saxony, $10-12

1952 message to Mrs. Romberger,

*"Fishing, clamming, swimming
In the ocean and the bay,
Judy, Barby, Lynne and Ming
Enjoying every day!*

*Daddy pays the bills
And takes time to remember
He'll see 'youall' in 2nd Church
On the 7th of September*

With best wishes, Henry & Family"

Babies

#8216-c. 1920, publisher unknown, $5-6

Things are shaping up nice here

#8215-c. 1920, publisher unknown, $5-6

EPILOGUE

Partners

I returned to the water this night
It was as I left it last
Still regal in its presence …
but lonelier now

The noise had left …
the vacations over
The ocean was solitude …
as it prefers to be in fall

A fine misty rain thickened the air …
perceptible only in the light from the lampposts
Warm moisture on my face …
womb temperature

I walked the silent boards …
attentive to my friend …
who seemed desperate for a human …
and pleased by my arrival

A boy entered the reverie
"Where do seagulls go at night?"
"Why isn't anyone playing in the sand?"
"What are those lights way out there?"

He rattled on
"How come all the windows are dark?"
"Can I have salt water taffy at Christmas time?"
"Where IS everybody?"

The voice of a child that was me …
embracing the wonderment …
ever captivated by this shore …
echoing in the timelessness of the surf

Tonight the mist anoints him …
King of Boardwalk—partner to the sea
Alone but one of many …
once the ocean whispers your name

Bibliography

Lost Lighthouses, Tim Harrison and Ray Jones, Globe Pequot Press, 2000

New Ideal State and County Survey and Atlas, Copyright 1916, Rand McNally & Co., Chicago

Steamboats Out of Baltimore, Robert H. Burgess and H. Graham Wood, Tidewater Publishers, Cambridge, Maryland, 1968